ABOUT THE AUTHOR

Monroe Mann, F.O.W.* is:

- the founder of Unstoppable Artists Business School in Manhattan
- the founder of Loco Dawn Films, LLC
- the author of a number of critically-acclaimed and publicly available books
- the producer/screenwriter/co-star of a number of films, including *In the Wake*, the world's first wakeboarding feature film, and *Fobbits*, the world's first comedic documentary about the war in Iraq
- a graduate of Dov Simens' Hollywood Film Institute and Digital Film Academy's 15-week filmmaking course
- a SAG, AFTRA, EQUITY Actor listed on IMDb, who has trained at American Academy of Dramatic Arts, Atlantic Theater Company, T. Schreiber Studios, Weist Barron, Endeavor Studios, Gene Frankel Theatre and Film Workshop, Scott Powers Productions, & School for Film & Television
- the lead singer and manager of the seven-piece R.O.M.P. band, *Running for Famous* (and co-creator and –producer of the upcoming television show of the same name.)
- a certified Guerrilla Marketing™ Coach, and the co-author of two upcoming business books with the famous Jay Conrad Levinson himself
- a graduate of Franklin College in Switzerland, with a degree in International Economics and French (with Honors)
- a graduate student at Pace University's Lubin School of Business in Manhattan (MBA Program) and at Western Carolina University's Master of Entrepreneurship program (ME Program)

- a combat veteran of Operation Iraqi Freedom (Intelligence Officer, and Military Intelligence Advisor to the 4th Iraqi Army) & former 'drill sergeant' at Officer Candidate School
- * F.O.W., i.e. Future Oscar® Winner, www.FutureOscarWinner. com ☺

OTHER RECOMMEND PROGRAMS

by Monroe Mann

- UABS Business Coaching & Classes
- MEM-CARDS: *The UABCs: Getting to the Top – Basic, Intermediate, & Advanced*
- BOOK: *Battle Cries for the Underdog – Fightin' Words for an Extraordinary Life*
- BOOK: *Operation: STARDOM, Books I - VI* (Business Book Series)
- BOOK: *Guerrilla Networking* (with Jay Conrad Levinson)
- BOOK: *Guerrilla Marketing for the Arts* (with Jay Conrad Levinson)
- BOOK: *To Benning & Back, Parts I, II, & III* (Military Book Series)

CRITICAL ACCLAIM OF FIRST EDITION OF *THE THEATRICAL JUGGERNAUT*

"A how-to for aspiring stars based on boot-camp persistence." – **CNN's Wolf Blitzer**

"This book may be just the antidote for an actor who has completely lost faith or given up control over his destiny." – **Backstage West, Los Angeles**

"Would I blurb your book? I would blurb your book to the skies! I have 33 books on my computer bookshelf. 32 are the ones I wrote. And the other? *The Theatrical Juggernaut.*" – **Jay Conrad Levinson, author of the *Guerrilla Marketing* series of books with over 14 million copies sold in 41 languages**

"*The Theatrical Juggernaut* is now required reading for every actor coming through our door." – **Doris Stinga, Funny Face Model & Talent**

"This is hands down THE best book on acting, or should I say business, that I have ever read! Forget all that crap that your college professors and other so-called 'experts', or 'Professionals' have told you about being an actor. This book at first seems so radical in its philosophy, yet upon reflection, so practical. What becomes apparent is that the ideas in this book are basically common sense! Monroe Mann has written a book that is so simple, direct, inspiring and empowering that one realizes that they have done themself a disservice by giving credence to all the conventional "wisdom" and the nay-sayers. I wish I had this book 10 years ago when I was just getting started! Once you read it yourself, you'll never feel at the mercy of the big fish again! Now what are you waiting for? Go get a copy, read it, and kick some butt!" – **Brett Owen, NY Acting Teacher**

"*The Theatrical Juggernaut* is a MUST for any actor. I even suggest it to veteran actor friends who have been successful in the entertainment business for 10 - 15 years as it will give you a lot of great ideas and useful tools to jump start your career. Besides helping boost my acting career, the book has really motivated me to produce some of my own projects like *The Bros.* and *Ticket Trouble* (www.tickettroublefilm. com)." – **Scott duPont, Actor, Producer, and State President, Florida Motion Picture & Television Association**, www.fmpta.org

"Monroe Mann shares with us the enormous gift of his optimism which only an exuberant and youthful spirit can provide. As a member of the Bar as well as a member of Equity, I truly appreciate the practice acdvice in *The Theatrical Juggernaut* written for unstoppable actors. His story of getting into the Cannes Film Festival is alone worth the price of this valuable book. Among the many magnificent quotes, my favorite is from his mother who only asks that you hire her son." – **Henry G. Miller, Entertainment Attorney; Clark, Gagliardi, & Miller**

"Monroe Mann is a young man who has done a lot of things in his 26 years. He's been to the inner circles of the Cannes Film Festival, started his own business, written several books, gotten a band together, produced an album and probably most importantly now, earned the rank of First Lieutenant in the National Guard. I've never met Monroe, but I have had the pleasure of communicating with him over the digital mail routes. I've also gotten a chance to read his terrific book, *The Theatrical Juggernaut*. That he is now training for deployment to a dangerous part of the world - he's been called to active duty - makes me proud to know him. But I'm only a little bit prouder - because, if this book is any indication of things to come, we are going to be hearing a lot about Monroe Mann. *The Theatrical Juggernaut* could be subtitled The Business ABC's of

Acting. This is a wonderful resource for any actor who wants to build a REAL career in this business. As a writer myself, I admire any one who actually manages to finish a book, much less someone who really has something to say - and Monroe has lots to say. He spares no `accepted wisdom' as he slams his points across with straight-forward, no nonsense style and a no-holds barred, take no prisoners approach to the acting business. There's advice in "Juggernaut" that will cause the timorous to quake and the cautious to question, but I can tell you from direct experience that his over-all message is one that every actor should take to heart. This is a business. Period. If you hope to be successful you must become a business-person. Monroe Mann's imprecations to pay attention to this oft-neglected part of your acting career are sometimes explosive and controversial but they are rarely off the mark. This is a book every actor should take an evening to read. Meanwhile, as we go about our daily lives over the next several months, each of us should stop every so often and give a thought to this generous, gifted and caring young man. Romp on, Monroe." – **Reviewed by Bob Fraser in his newsletter, Hollywood How-To. Bob is an Emmy-recognized actor, writer, director, and producer, & the author of *You Must Act!* www. ShowBizHowTo.com**

"*The Theatrical Juggernaut: The Psyche Of The Star* by Monroe Mann (founder and president of Unstoppable Artists Business School) is a practical, straightforward, no-nonsense book on the subject of pursing acting as a career. Rather than exhaustively address such standard matters as finding good headshots, creating a monologue, or getting an agent, it focuses intensely on why 99% of aspiring actors never even get noticed, and why the overwhelming majority of aspiring performers are in the wrong line of work. As for the few who are in the right line suited to their talents, *The Theatrical Juggernaut* explains how the need for an industry "break" to achieve success is a myth, and why everything rests squarely on one's own shoulders. An absolute "must" for anyone seriously considering or pursuing a career in acting." – **Midwest Book Review**

"I talk about your book in almost every class I teach." – **Jim Bonney, Actor, & NY Acting Teacher**

"Here's a book that promises to encourage our aspiring young actors. Full of ideas, no luck involved, hard work, and best of all, the courage to go out there and act on it. Acting is an art which this reviewer could never quite achieve. It's a slap on the back, good fellow, and nothing matters except the 'play's the thing.' Timely advice for young actors who are just ready to fly in the wings of the stage. Yet Mann writes the warning, 'You have to decide which group you are in… If you aren't among those who are doing everything within their power to reach their goals, then you are among the losers, the wannabes, the quitters, the pretenders.' This writer is not an actor. The goals outlined in *The Theatrical Juggernaut* can be applied to any life as it begins. To work hard, in earnest, without quitting. Without being discouraged. Honorable work without criticism and knowing what's possible by trying is the real message for all of us. I have been inspired as any young person would be."
– **Shenandoah University, Parent's Guide to Children's Media**

"This guy is one of the best. This book is a must read for any performing artist! Even if you don't have an interest in the arts, this book can motivate you to reach your dreams. Monroe Mann is the "Tony Robbins" for the new generation! GET THIS BOOK IF YOU ARE A SERIOUS ACTOR!" – **Christopher Lucas, Actor, and Author,** *Secrets of Show Business Success*

"I purchased this book YEARS ago, and it has been a favorite of mine ever since! *The Theatrical Juggernaut* is one of the most influential, most inspiring books ever written about the business of show. Monroe Mann does not pull any punches with this one; straight and to-the-point, Mr. Mann exposes many truths about the industry and explains quite simply that show business is business, pure and simple. It is his belief in these two principles of Attitude & Business Sense that is making Monroe Mann a huge success and a recognized name in the artistic and business world. For those of you who are looking for an opportunity that can positively change your life, pick up this book and read it with an open mind. Then take the next step and DO what it teaches. The tools you will learn will bring your career to new heights!" – **Greg Cilmi, Actor, & Founder, Well Urned Productions,** www.WellUrnedProductions.com

"Everything about this book is a testament to Mann's life concept: *You can get anything you want out of life.* Focused on acting, *The Theatrical Juggernaut* is a ridiculously insightful and inspirational acting handbook. It's the kind of book that pulls you in two directions - on one hand, you're drawn in by Mann's stories and advice, and on the other hand, you feel like you need to be getting out there, whoopin' some theatrical ass. It's an honest book that makes the reader take responsibility for life decisions. In reading this book, one realizes the detriment of blaming others for one's failures. In all, this is a fantastic book written by a man who refuses to back down from anything. His work, attitude, and persistence are truly inspirational." – **Daniel 'Reed' Thrall, Lead Singer, Redlands,** www.DanielThrall.com

"Dear Monroe Mann. I don't know you, but I've read your book, and it is AWESOME. You and I have some similar thoughts about this business and it was really nice to see it finally put into words. I couldn't agree more. I'm redoubling my efforts to become the movie star that I knew I'd become ever since I was a wee kid doing impressions for my relatives in the living room. I'll keep my eye out for you when we're both at the top, and someday, I'm gonna shake your hand and say thanks in person. Oh, and about that Oscar… RACE YA!" – **Bobby Timony, Actor,** www. TwinComics.com

"Monroe Mann's book, *The Theatrical Juggernaut,* is a fine work, inspirational, tough-minded, and with the down and dirty information an actor needs to get off his rear end and accomplish his dreams." – **RJ Lewis, The One-Man Vaudeville Show, Magician and Actor,** www.ArJayEnt.com

"The book you wrote for actors is the most information, and motivating book that I have EVER read. I have read dozens of books that are supposed to help the actor, but NONE come close to the clear-cut book you so brilliantly wrote for actors. I now see my career in a whole new light, and I can actually see that my being a success is within my power. Thanks." - **Ginger Leilani, Actress,** www.GingerLeilani.com

"Monroe Mann's inspirational book, *The Theatrical Juggernaut*, dispels the myth that Hollywood and its agents and managers control the careers of performing artists. Tying in with the entrepreneurial spirit that helped build America, Monroe reminds 'actors' that they are really venture capital businessmen (and women) who hold the key to their own destinies! He challenges performers not to wait for the golden career to drop in their laps, but to forge their own path and dare to create the careers they dare to dream of!" – **Daphne Shawn, Actress,** www.DaphneShawn.com

"*The Theatrical Juggernaut* was probably the single most inspiring text I've read to kick my attitude and acting career into high gear. It reminded me of many things I'd forgotten about, and introduced me to new concepts I'd never thought of—which seemed so obvious after the blinders had been pulled back." – **Erik Davies, Actor,** www.ErikDavies.com

"A friend of mine said 'Jeff, you have to check out this site… UnstoppableArtists.com; it's right up your alley.' So I checked it out, liked what I saw, and made plans in my head to call Monroe & take his class. I also purchased his book *The Theatrical Juggernaut* and started reading it. Wow! There I was, going through the motions that every wannabe actor does: sending out headshots, hoping, wishing, crossing my fingers that one day my dreams would come true… and then I got smacked in the face from reading *The Theatrical Juggernaut* by Monroe Mann. Boy, was I dense! I finally got it: I had to *make* things happen. I started practicing what Monroe preached, and not only did I get results, but my confidence, energy and self-worth just soared! Talk about motivation — I felt totally empowered after just the first chapter. Thanks to his book, and practicing what it preached, I ended up signing with my first legit agent here in New York. You see, I had just auditioned for a legit agent who was very interested in me but who explained that he had two other actors who were 'my type', who always booked for them. But he kept my headshots and said, 'You never know what might change.' Well, after reading *The Theatrical Juggernaut*, I felt so "Unstoppable" that I wrote a letter to this agent, included movie tickets, and told him to go to the movies and spot roles that he could have cast me in. A couple of days later he called, informing me that he was going to sign me. Using the guerrilla tactics stated in the book, I signed with legit agent Barry

Kolker of The Carson Organization on March 25, 2003. If I hadn't read Monroe's book I would not have an agent right now.'" – **Jeff Goldstein, Actor,** www.JeffGoldstein.com

"Monroe is all about accountability and active, positive attitudes. He's right, no one can make this - or anything - happen in this life except you. His classes and books are the kick in the pants that every actor needs in order to reverse their humble modest way of approaching their careers with, "I hope I am good enough." – **Jeanette Bonner, Actress,** www.JeanetteBonner.com

"Halfway through my freshman year in college, I became frustrated with the whole acting process. I was majoring in drama. I felt like I was wasting my time and money doing nothing and not learning what I felt I really needed to know about the business aspects of a career in entertainment—I was losing confidence fast. Somehow I came across *The Theatrical Juggernaut* online and HAD to read it. The hope that resulted simply from purchasing the book online right then and there enabled me to continue what I was doing. ...then of course I READ the book, and things are just a million times better now too! The book is amazing, I learned so much and it helped to boost my confidence and self-esteem dramatically. Monroe's "go-get-'em" attitude is just what any struggling artist needs to perservere and be fabulous. Get back on track and read this book!" – **Elysia Segal, Actress,** www.ElysiaSegal.com

"What Monroe Mann has provided with *The Theatrical Juggernaut,* is the how to manual for those who want to control their careers, written by one who is. The majority of actors out there, and people in general for that matter, tend to wait for their careers, their lives, to happen to them. Many drift about halfheartedly and wait for the currents of fate to change. They fail to see that in order to succeed you cannot hide behind excuses and sidestep personal responsibility. Monroe Mann teaches you how to demand this responsibility, how to take control of your career and place that weight squarely on your own shoulders. In doing so you become driven with purpose and find that each step taken towards your goal resounds with self-empowerment. If you are in any way serious about your career reading this book is one decision you cannot afford not to make. It is after all your career." – **Ian Kerch, Actor**

"Awesome, amazing, life-changing! After finding it in a book store, I flipped through 'TTJ' and was so grabbed by Mann's powerful style of writing that I couldn't put it down! I finished *Theatrical Juggernaut* in the bookstore before I could bring myself to stop reading, buy it and finish it at home! This book will teach you more than any "Marketing for Actors" class in a shorter period of time. Buy now!" – **Tamara Kosh, Actress**

"This book is FABULOUS and for anyone out there who is struggling, who is barely making it, or who is successful beyond imagination—you must have this book. There are some wonderful ideas/hints that have really helped me and I am now ready to get out there and make my dream come true! As you say Monroe, "Romp On!"" – **Mindy Raymond, Actress**

"I picked up this book on a whim and was happily surprised. Unlike other 'How to Be an Actor' books, this book is a motivational tool. Monroe really is the Tony Robbins of the entertainment biz. I have felt a renewed sense of direction and power over my life since reading this book. Everything that Monroe says is right on the money and he gives the reader a great lookout on everyday aspects of our lives. If you haven't read this or Monroe's other book *To Benning and Back*, pick them both up and get motivated today. ... The man is like 25 and is accomplishing big things. He doesn't just talk the talk, he runs full speed to his goals." —**Nikki Switzer, Actress**

"In a profession where so many say, 'You Can't', Monroe Mann says, 'You Can!' *The Theatrical Juggernaut - The Psyche of the Star* is the manifesto for actors everywhere who want to leave doubt and negativity behind, and who want to start taking an active part in fulfilling their artistic dreams. This book inspired me to go beyond the conventional, and to approach the business of acting with the same kind of passion and enthusiasm that I have for the craft!" – **Joe Whelski, Actor**

"This book should be required reading for anyone thinking of making acting a CAREER, not a hobby. The odds against a successful acting career are tantamount to an Immoveable Object, and they must be overcome with UNSTOPPABLE Force. This book will either spur you to succeed or save you thousands of dollars in wasted time and energy. Some of its precepts are slightly controversial, but most of the material is solid, helpful and encouraging...and the quote section and bibliography is worth the price alone." – **Ken Kupstis, Actor**

"Monroe tells the TRUTH about the business without the sugar-coating. Along with sound advice, he provides inspiration and the positive reinforcement that all actors need. Whether you're a beginner looking for direction or a veteran needing a 'charge,' *The Theatrical Juggernaut* delivers." – **Vincent Prezioso, Actor**

"I read your book three times and love the thing… Thanks for having the balls to do what you're doing and inspiring countless numbers of people. I will beat you to the top." – **Jim Tierney, Actor**

"To everyone who doubts what Monroe says in this book, get ready to eat dirt because YOU will be left behind and be unemployed. Monroe has accomplished more in a few years than most 'actors' who have been 'in the business' for decades. What he says is bare-bones, no-nonsense, NO EXCUSES, to the point truth about making a career in show BUSINESS and that is exactly the point: It's all about business. Yet most actors have no business sense, hence the high rate of pessimism, bitterness, and unemployment. You really want to be an actor? THEN GET OFF YOUR BUTT and make it happen. END OF STORY. If you aren't successful, then you didn't REALLY want it in the first place and the only person to blame is you! There are massive amounts of information and motivation in this book. It may be just what you need to jumpstart your attitude and career. That's what I needed and now my future is a blaze of hope and promise! The same can be true for you. HOOAH!" – **Craig Rehnke, Actor**

"*The Theatrical Juggernaut* is a book that needs to be in the hands of all actors—all artists for that matter—who want to build a successful and fruitful career in the arts. In a no-nonsense, butt-kicking, yet refreshingly encouraging style, Monroe Mann explains the importance of being more than an artist; that becoming a well informed and competent businessman/woman is absolutely necessary. Warning: You cannot read this book without realizing that your career is in your own hands and yours alone and that your hard work is what will make or break it. Period. This book drops the responsibility for your career right in your own lap. It leaves you with no possible excuses for 'failure'. *The Theatrical Juggernaut* is about how business sense, hard work and a good attitude toward the process are the building blocks for success—not luck or talent alone. I believe this book should be given to every student of the arts wishing to come to New York or Hollywood and 'make it'. It explains the difference between hoping your career will happen and making it happen. It's a gift of a book!" – **Unknown Reviewer on Amazon.com**

"This book is a true inspiration. It is TRUTH, EMPOWERMENT, and ADRENALINE all in one, and it keeps your momentum going, which we all need from time to time. It gives you tangible information to help you move your career along at a very brisk pace. EVERY actor (every PERSON) MUST read this book! I'm going to read it again, and again, and again." – **Marian Massaro, Actress**

"He lives what he writes about." – **Susan Crozzoli, Actress**

"I just want to say thank you. Since buying your book in January, your attitude has been contagious. I live in LA and I subscribe to your newsletters. My roommate has read your book. My friend gets the newsletters as well. There are inspirational quotes from your book strategically places around our apartment. I now read *Entrepreneur Magazine*. I send out postcards like never before. And a dozen other things. And when I'm down, I just read the right words that I need to hear to kick me in the butt again: *The Theatrical Juggernaut*. I know that Unstoppable Artists didn't do this for me. I'm doing everything under my own power and my own way. But I gotta say that UABS was definitely a contributing factor in my positive decision making. Your word is spreading like wildfire. Like I said, it's contagious. Thank you again for the many kicks in the butt, and the many more awaiting me in the future!" – **Greg Vojtanek, Actor**

"Monroe's book should be the handbook for all actors who actually want to make a living at acting! – **Julie Delman, Actress**

The Theatrical Juggernaut (The Psyche of the Star)

2nd Edition, Director's Cut

Monroe Mann

Bloomington, IN  Milton Keynes, UK

authorHOUSE®

AuthorHouse™
1663 Liberty Drive, Suite 200
Bloomington, IN 47403
www.authorhouse.com
Phone: 1-800-839-8640

AuthorHouse™ UK Ltd.
500 Avebury Boulevard
Central Milton Keynes, MK9 2BE
www.authorhouse.co.uk
Phone: 08001974150

First published by AuthorHouse 11/21/2006

ISBN: 1-4259-6780-9 (sc)

Library of Congress Control Number: 2006908781

Printed in the United States of America
Bloomington, Indiana

This book is printed on acid-free paper.

DEDICATION

My mother and family have always been my primary sources of inspiration. I dedicate this book to all my fellow actors (and mavericks everywhere) bravely pursuing their dreams. I hope that this book can be to you what my family is to me. I look forward to meeting you at the top.

ACKNOWLEDGEMENTS
FROM 1st EDITION
(Slightly Edited)

(This is a precursor to my Oscar speech)

I thank my mother and father for buying this computer on which I'm writing this book. If you hadn't done so, Unstoppable Artists Business School might never have come to be. Thanks so much for helping me get both my acting business, and my business school, off the ground.

I thank my mother, though, especially for being my biggest fan, for always believing in *all* that I have chosen to do, and for never following through with your numerous threats to kick me out of the house. Thank you madam, queen of all women, and fountain of endless encouragement. Thanks for listening.

Thanks to my sisters, Emily and Hilary, for both encouraging me and making fun of me; it has all helped to inspire me. Yeah, well, he's on TV. That's right!

Emily insisted on a paragraph of her own, so here it is. Hil, I hope you don't mind.

I thank Dennis O'Neil, for casting me as Alan Strang in *Equus*, and giving me the courage and confidence to actually decide to pursue a career in acting. You and that review have irrevocably determined my fate: "A totally amazing performance by young Monroe Mann... a standing ovation on stilts," wrote the *Conway Daily Sun*, in North Conway, New Hampshire about my performance at the Equity-approved Eastern Slope Playhouse. That review wouldn't have happened without you!

I also want to thank the wonderful cast of *Equus*. To this day I have not been with a more talented and professional group of people. Were it not for *Equus*, I would not be where I am today.

I thank Roberta Muse, my high school French teacher, for being my first and favorite fan outside the family. Thank you to Dr. Christopher Matthews, my bloke from Franklin, for your wonderful friendship, words of wisdom over the years, and the groovy card that has kept me going when times were rough: "Next stop: Broadway!"

Thanks to *One Life to Live* director Joe Contugno for telling me point blank that I have what it takes. Thanks to Sig De Miguel, of Mackey-Sandrich Casting, for being my first real industry contact in New York. Thanks to Amanda Mackey Johnson for giving me the opportunity to intern at your office. Thanks to Mary Egan of Liz Lewis Casting for never giving up on me after my failing to book audition after audition. Thanks to John Cole and Kristen Garver of New York City Opera for the great times and music. Thanks to friend, Chad Kimball, for never looking down on me because I wasn't as far along as you were. Thanks to friend, Markus Leonard, Mr. Quick View, for conveniently starting your business at the same time as me, and helping me come up with great ideas along the way. Thanks to Gail Williams for being the nicest agent I've met to date. Thanks to friend, Jen Hamilton, for not becoming the president of my fan club, for we both know that wouldn't have worked out.

Thanks to Franklin College, for giving me the most incredible education and enlightenment I could ever have received in only two years. You have opened me up to new ideas, people, cultures, and languages, and moreover, helped me to realize that acting is my destiny. Thanks to my wonderful professors and friends, and especially Duncan Autrey.

Thanks to friend Daniel Reed for creating the beautiful acoustic guitar arrangements and vocal harmonies that I often listened to while writing this book. Your songs have inspired me to drive and drive and drive and drive and drive. Ray Sullivan, you weenie, thanks for never calling me back! Chas Crawford, thanks for molding me into what I am today. Thanks to WPLS, 96.5, "The *Best* Alternative," for giving me confidence, and for letting me play *The Beach Boys* every once in a while.

On that note, thanks to *The Beach Boys* for making my life an endless summer. I'm one of your biggest fans.

Thanks to the Blackwell Hall, Furman University, American University, and Fryeburg Academy gangs for helping me to mature. Richard Askew, where are you?

Believe it or not, I thank every one out there who thinks I'm a horrible actor, who thinks I'm going to fail, who never cast me in a high school play, who tells me I'm wasting my time, and who has no faith in the power of the human spirit. Each time you tell me I can't, you fuel my passion to prove to myself that I can. Each time I succeed, I have much to thank you for.

On the flip side, thanks to all the people who actually *do* have faith in people's dreams, and my dream in particular of winning an Oscar. When my friends believe that I'm going to win that Oscar, it makes the reality of achieving it all the more easier to believe myself.

Thanks to everyone who has cast me in their films and shows and helped me to build a resume that I am very much proud of, especially Mike Miley, Marc Toscano, and Eric Walkuski. Hey Eric: It's gonna be nice!

Thanks to all my clients for allowing me to help you kick some major theatrical butt. I look forward to seeing all of you at the top! Thanks especially to Christopher Patrick Lucas, for trusting me enough to be my first client, and for being the first to call me the "Tony Robbins of the Acting World."

Thanks to the United States Army, the New York Army National Guard, my drill sergeants, and my TAC officers, for creating in me the knowledge that anything is possible, despite one's current mental or physical condition.

Likewise, thanks to Tom Hanks and the cast of *Saving Private Ryan*, and Pauly Shore and the cast of *In the Army Now*, for making me realize what a sacrifice our military has made for the freedoms we today take for granted. You were my recruiters. Thanks SGT Lippy.

Thanks to Cynthia Kersey, and her book, *Unstoppable*, and the wonderfully inspiring story of Mr. Legson Kayira contained therein.

After reading about what obstacles you overcame, Mr. Kayira, I know that I can do anything.

Thanks to everyone at Guerrilla Marketing International for publishing the most enlightening and helpful business books I have ever read.

Thanks to Dan Snow at Unlimited Publishing for making this book a published reality, and for once again proving to me that if you want to do something, just go out there and find some way to do it.

Thanks to my entertainment attorney, George Sheanshang, for looking after my best interests. Thanks to Henry Miller for referring me.

Thanks to Garis Publicity Agency in Los Angeles for your insight and assistance. You don't realize how you have encouraged me.

Finally, thanks be to God, my lord and savior, Jesus Christ. That *Bible* of yours... now *that's* inspiration!

ACKNOWLEDGEMENTS TO 2nd EDITION, DIRECTOR'S CUT

First off, thanks again to God, Jesus, mom, dad, Em, & Hil. You guys rock!

Hilary, a big congrats to you on your stellar reviews in *AM New York* and the *New York Times* for your knockout performance in the film *Vacationland*.

Emily, thanks for being my friend, and for all of your support and encouragement. It's always a treat when you stop by. Bring food! ☺

Mom, thank you *so* much for pestering and encouraging me non-stop to go to business school and get my Masters. If it weren't for you, I would never have taken the GMAT, applied to schools, earned a scholarship, or secured government loans. And now, I am a grad student at two different schools earning both titles of Master of Entrepreneurship, as well as Master of Business Administration. Thanks to you. I love you mom!

Dad (& mom), thank you for so much for being so supportive of my dreams as I continue my trek to the top of show business. It'll come back to you tenfold. While in Iraq, my motto was "Stay Alive in 2005!". This year, "Hits & Chicks in 2006." Next year? "Live like Heaven in 2007." That includes a condo for me and a new house for you! And of course, in 2007, my feature film *In the Wake* is going to be going into pre-production. Yippee!

Thanks to Em, Hil, Greg, & Steve Chiarello particularly, for helping me survive my latest debilitating emotional breakdown. This business is *killer*, and were it not for your amazing support and assistance, I am not sure I would have found the strength to continue.

A huge thanks to Jay Conrad Levinson. Your friendship and support helped keep my spirits up through an entire war, and I am ever grateful for your ongoing assistance with everything. I am *so* excited to be writing two books with you. What an honor. And thank you for *your* service, my fellow army intelligence officer.

Thanks to students Scot Wisnieski, Jeff Goldstein, Doug Williams, Sheryl Matthys, JP Richards, Brett Duggan, Phil Estrera, Tamara Kosh, Eva Gil, Mateo Moreno, Danielle Ozymandias, and countless others for helping me to run the school over the years, and for all of your wonderful ideas that have kept the fire brightly lit within me for so many years.

Thanks to Bones Rodriguez, Bob Fraser, Mike Finnell, Lorraine Serabian (Tony Nominee!) & Joan Ellis (Tony Nominee!) for your help with the school.

Thanks to Greg Cilmi, Tracy Ransome, and Michael Schreiber for your assistance in helping me get my business open again upon my return from Iraq in November 2005, and for your assistance with the Mem-Card decks. The school would not have expanded and improved as quickly without your insight and assistance. I wish each of you the best and much success.

Thanks to all those who (oh so wisely) became clients and student of the school upon my return from Iraq, including Nicole Moeller, Leigh Montanye, Jenn Star, Tom Abraham, Amanda Rowan, Ashley Serafin, Dennis Hurley, Angela Billings, Margie Fabon, Don Pravda, Christel Ferguson, Marcia Harp, Colie Crutcher, Renee Manning, Tracy Ransome, Greg Cilmi, Michael Schreiber, Natasha Hanina, Travis Love, Diana De La Cruz, and Chad V. Holtcamp. You guys make it all worthwhile.

Thanks to everyone who helped with ideas for this new edition of this book, especially, Evander Duck, Rick Olmos, Ana Cronin, Madalyn McKay, Tracy Ransome, Michael Schreiber, Greg Cilmi, Jeff Goldstein, Doug Williams, Brett Duggan, Phil Estrera, & Scot Wisniewski. And let's not forget all of the wonderful people who said such wonderful (and true!) things about *The Theatrical Juggernaut* in the front of this book.

Thanks to all of my readers, students, friends, fans, and enemies for making my life so interesting. Thanks especially to everyone who has helped encourage me to continue my dreams of expanding the school nationally, and then internationally. I truly do appreciate the support, and you're a constant reminder to me that no great accomplishments are realized without the help of others. When I get to the top, and I am on *Inside the Actor's Studio*, I will be asked, "How did you do it?" I look forward to responding, "I did it all by myself… with the help of hundreds of other people!"

Thanks to Dan Snow & Unlimited Publishing, as well as the team at AuthorHouse for making this book a reality.

Thanks to Dominic at the Drama Book Shop for agreeing to be the first book store to stock this book back in 2001, and to Eleanor, Jessica, Freddy, Matthew, Rick, and the rest of the fantastic staff at DBS for helping the book continue its journey towards an Oscar. I mean Pulitzer. ☺

Finally, thanks to *The Theatrical Juggernaut, 1st Edition* for helping me get as far as I have. See 'Introduction to 2nd Edition' for details and explanation. ☺

ABOUT UNSTOPPABLE ARTISTS BUSINESS SCHOOL

Unstoppable Artists Business School is the world's only business school for artists. We focus on the two factors that have the biggest impact on success: Attitude; and Business Sense. Finally... a school for artists that offers you the business skills and savvy to complement your talents. Unstoppable Artists Business School was formed for one reason: to show people that they can succeed in the arts. Someone has to be the next star. Why not you?

What started as the motivational consulting firm Unstoppable Actors back in 1999, has now morphed into Unstoppable Artists Business School, the one and only true business school for artists in the world, run by and for artists, *part-time*.

It is run part-time because we are all out there kicking some artistic butt, in some way shape or form. We are completely and totally obsessed with success. In fact, if we aren't at the top yet... you might *want* to hold your breath; We'll be there shortly. In fact, by the time you are reading this book, we may already have arrived. ☺

This company was not formed as an alternative to acting & the arts; rather, it was formed as a supplement. And so it remains today. We *are going* to make it big, or die trying. It's as simple as that. We are 100% bitterness-free, and this school has no intention of closing once management reaches celebrity status. In other words, the school is not just a 'day job' until we reach the top. It's actually the other way around: the artistic world is our day job, and teaching others is what we do on the side... because we love teaching just as much. It is said that those who can, *do*, and those who can't, *teach*. I think there's one part missing from that axiom: Those who can **do** AND **teach**... DO BOTH!

Our aim is to inspire and guide actors & artists of all disciplines; to help them reach their true potential through attitude- and business-focused courses, coaching, mentoring, books, and products.

There are artists... and then there are Unstoppable Artists. Which would you rather be?

Meet you at the top!

INTRODUCTION TO FIRST EDITION

A juggernaut as defined by Merriam Webster's Collegiate Dictionary is "a massive inexorable force, campaign, movement, or object that crushes whatever is in its path." Thus, a theatrical juggernaut would be an unstoppable actor that lets nothing get in the way of success.

In all sincerity, we at Unstoppable Artists Business School are of the belief that if you really want something, you do it and get it done, regardless of the situation and despite any odds. If you don't get what you "want", it's because deep down, you really didn't want it in the first place. Think about that. Stop, for a moment, and think about that. Consider your own life. What you really wanted, you found a way of getting. Surprising?

It's time to start taking responsibility for your career. We believe that if you *really* want to get cast, you will. We believe that if you *really* want to get in the unions, you will find a way. We believe that if you *really* want to be on Broadway or become a Hollywood star, you *will* figure out the way.

If you want to succeed, here is our oh-so-secret and guarded formula for success: GO DO IT! Stop making excuses and start making progress! Just suck it up and drive on. And if by some chance you don't succeed, there's only one person to blame. That's right. You!

Once, at a SAG Film Society screening, an individual began his introduction to the audience with the following words: "In this business in which we have no control over our futures..." Whoa!

The blame for this person's failure is always on something *else*, and never on himself. Just because *he* has succumbed to defeat and decided that the business was too much for him doesn't mean that *everyone* is bitter.

Some of us know that we are going to succeed. Some of us are determined to make it. Some of us refuse to quit. Some of us are of the volition that our destinies are *ours* for the making.

Bottom line, it comes down to a simple distinction: Some among us are dilettantes dabbling in a field of dreams, with no clear goals, no definable plans, no motivation, and a pitiful attitude. What are the others?

Unstoppable Artists.

Which would you rather be?

Read on…

INTRODUCTION TO 2nd EDITION, DIRECTOR'S CUT

In the acknowledgements, I said 'thank you' to the first edition of this book. Why, you ask?

Well, you see, on July 17, 2001—two weeks prior to the original release of the first edition of *TTJ*—I decided I would write the introduction to the 2nd Edition. You see, success is all about forethought.

Well, this is what I wrote, verbatim. I added the bold and underline for a reason, as you will soon see:

"Well, it's been but one year since I wrote *The Theatrical Juggernaut*. In that short time, **I've put into practice everything about which I wrote**, and have since signed with William Morris Agency; hired Garis Publicity Agency; booked four national commercials, each grossing at least $15,000; appeared over ten times in seven feature films, one of which might lead to an Oscar nomination for Best Supporting Actor; **appeared on 100 radio talk shows**, and over 12 television shows, to include Letterman, Conan, Leno, Geraldo, Sally Jesse Raphael, and Politically Incorrect; **written another book (on military life)**; written and sold a screenplay that is now being produced into a major motion picture; achieved the rank of red belt (Red, Brown, Black) at Tiger Schulmann's Karate; **learned to swing dance like a pro**; expanded my business Unstoppable Actors to include ten additional consultants and a groovy midtown central office; **become totally fluent in French; reasonably so in Italian; run my platoon in the Army National Guard; been accepted to Army Intelligence School; learned to do a Tantrum on a wakeboard;** and finally, I've become a millionaire through acting, book sales, and my consulting business."

Remember: I wrote this two weeks BEFORE the first edition of *The Theatrical Juggernaut* was released. Pretty ambitious, right? This was in 2001. I was 22 years old. A little overambitious even? Completely unreasonable and unrealistic, don't you think? I don't think so.

You see, take a look at the bold and underlined text you just read. Bold means that I did exactly that. Underline means I am nearly there. For instance, at this writing, William Morris and I are talking about me being signed to their agency as an actor, screenwriter and producer for my film, *In the Wake*. Also, while I never hired Garis Publicity on retainer, since writing that, I have had four other publicists on various retainers. As for booking four commercials, I have not yet done that, but my foresight has resulted in representation by Ingber & Associates for commercials. Regarding my acceptance to Army Intelligence School, I not only did that, but also went through the most difficult of crucibles as a deployed combat soldier in Iraq. I could go on.

What's my point, you ask? I have two points I am trying to make:

First, write down your future. You might be surprised that it comes true pretty much exactly as you wrote it down.

Second, and more importantly... the stuff in this book WORKS, and works WELL! I know *exactly* what I am talking about when it comes to teaching people about success through attitude and business sense. I absolutely guarantee you that if you put the techniques in this book into practice, you will soon see your wildest dreams coming true right before your very eyes.

Sure, not everything that I envisioned and planned for has unfolded *exactly* as intended (some things happened sooner; other things I am still moving towards), but the bottom line that I am trying to make is this—and read this carefully—*I have either accomplished or nearly accomplished everything I wrote down about my future on July 17th, 2001.* You can do the same thing for your life and career. It really isn't that hard. Here are the three steps:

1. Read this book
2. Do what it says
3. Become a success.

Simple!

WHY I WROTE THIS BOOK

Spring 1998. I am sitting in my room in France, in my French family's home. I am there studying French and living like a real Frenchman. I do, however, take showers daily. ☺

It is the summer of my junior year of college. I have one more year to go, and I know, without a doubt, that I am going to pursue acting as soon as I graduate.

I am in the city of Hyeres, on the French Riviera, and but an hour drive from the city of Cannes, and the famed Cannes Film Festival (which would be starting in a few weeks).

I am reading a whole slew of books that I bought on Amazon.com. Each book is about how to succeed as an actor; how to get booked in commercials; how to get an agent; how to—How To—HOW TO!

'How to' what, though? I am surprised as I am reading them that they aren't all subtitled, "How to get Really Depressed and Give Up Before You Start," or "How to Inculcate Yourself With Feelings of Self-Doubt about a Career in Show Biz," or even, "Your Chances of Success are Slim to None—So Give Up Now." Truly, I feel miserable as I am reading these books. Books that purportedly were going to pump me up and instill within me the confidence to go after my dreams are making me more and more depressed with every turn of the page.

Every single one of these books is telling me that I should do it for the art, not the money; that I am probably not going to be one of the 'lucky ones'; that if I'd be happy doing anything else, I should just quit now.

"SCREW YOU!" I am thinking. "Who they hell are you to tell me what I can and can't do?! Why are you telling me before I even start that I can't do it? This is the most difficult business in the world! You should be telling me that I can do it! That I have what it takes! That it's going to happen!"

Well, I vowed that summer, in May 1998 in southern France, that I was one-day going to write my own book on the subject, and that it would be the total anti-thesis of all of these books. This book—I decided—would become known as the most inspiring book for actors ever written. This book would help scores of actors just like me realize that we indeed *do* have what it takes to get to the top, and that with the right attitude, success on any scale would be possible. Since no book existed that was going to encourage me to go after an Oscar and a Tony... I decided—against all odds—that I was going to write it myself.

Fast Forward: Summer 1999, two months after graduating from college... I sat down and wrote the back cover to the very book you have in your hands. Take a moment to re-read it. Now get this: I had no true experience as a professional actor, and no experience as a published author. Yeah! I wrote the back cover to the book (virtually verbatim as you see it) before I even had the credibility to write the book. In fact, I ended up publishing the book before I really had any credibility to do so. That's what success is all about: breaking the rules. But the truth is that I did have *something*. What I had was faith, ambition, chutzpah, and what had by then become a complete and total obsession.

Despite being laughed at by agents, ridiculed by my peers, and questioned by my friends and family, I did what few people truly do: I persevered, and found solutions to my perceived problems.

Fast Forward Again: Two years later, in July 2001, *The Theatrical Juggernaut – The Psyche of the Star* was published. At first, no book stores would stock it. But that's not an excuse, just a delay. Some of you may have heard this story in some shape or form. I did what any future superstar would do: I took matters into my own hands. I found the guts within me to stand on the sidewalk outside Drama Book Shop in Times Square in Manhattan and peddle my wares to actors coming in and going out of the building. With a killer product and a killer sales pitch, I managed to sell it to about 1 out of every 4th person who passed by.

Everything was going really well until some rude guy came up to me and said, "What do you think you're doing?"

"I'm selling my book," I replied, rather perturbed with this interruption to my selling machine.

"Well, you can't sell it here," he said, in what I felt was a very inappropriate tone. "It's illegal."

"Oh yeah? Well who are you anyway," I replied.

His response shook away any haughtiness I may have been exhibiting.

"Me? I'm Dominic, the manager of Drama Book Shop! And I am about to call the cops."

I was floored. Speechless. I became so nervous. I realized that my master plan that was going so well... had just crumbled before my very eyes. Just as my book selling business was about to take off... it was floored. Grounded. Terminated. It was all over.

But wait! Maybe it wasn't... In what felt like a decade, but what must have been but a few moments, I came up with a response that would forever change the future of *The Theatrical Juggernaut* and my life.

"What if I told you that I just sold over 50 copies of my book in less than two hours to your very own customers and that part of future sales could be yours?"

His demeanor changed almost instantly. A wry smile came across his face.

"Well, in that case, please come up to my office."

Well, ladies and gents, since that momentous day, my first book, *The Theatrical Juggernaut* has—just as I had intended back in 1998—indeed become one of the best-selling 'how to succeed as an actor' books of all time. It has also been called by reader after reader... 'the most inspiring book on how to succeed as an actor ever written'. And I am proud to now be known in many circles as 'the Tony Robbins of the Acting & Artistic World'.

What am I trying to say? Just two things:

A) Thanks for picking up this second edition. It means more to me than you know.

B) You are UNSTOPPABLE and nothing is in your way (if you truly believe it to be so).

HOW TO USE THIS BOOK

Read this book with an open mind! That is first and foremost. You are about to be told many things you may never have been told before. In writing this book, I have broken a lot of rules, and so be it. You must keep an open mind. If you examine everything I say with a fresh slate, you will find what I say far easier to grasp and far less frustrating to read.

The Theatrical Juggernaut is broken down into three sections. Part A stresses the psychological requirements of a successful actor, whereas Part B includes a number of 'How To' Guides that will help you start translating the psychological aspects of Part A into tangible results. In Part C is the annex, which includes our reading list, the top characteristics of unstoppable people, my famous 'Cannes' story, The Agent Matrix, and some other goodies.

While this book may be begun anywhere, as each chapter is self-contained, it is meant to be read straight through. If there is a certain chapter that intrigues you, you may want to start there, but be sure to come back and start from the beginning at some point.

By the time you finish this book, you will be on your way to becoming an Unstoppable Artist. Your mentality is going to be very optimistic, and you are going to feel quite different from when you started. You are going to look at yourself, this business, and your career in a whole new light.

Countless readers have told me that their copy of the first edition is nearly entirely yellow now because of all of the sentences they highlighted. So, just as I recommended in the first edition, have a pen or pencil, or better yet, a highlighter, handy while you are reading, and highlight the sentences, quotes, and sections that inspire you most. You will certainly find a lot of them. Refer to them often. Take notes in the margin. Mark up the book as if your future depended on it (it sorta does!)

Once you've finished the book, I absolutely guarantee that you are going to want to read over everything again with your new Unstoppable mentality guiding the way. There are many parts that you will benefit from reading a second and third time, so pick up this book and read it again when finished!

In fact, whenever you are bummed, open up this book. Whenever you are thinking of quitting, take this book from your bookshelf. Whenever you are downtrodden, discouraged, feeling rejected, depressed, bitter, or just STUCK and getting nowhere, open this book and start reading it again.

I once read about a man who wrote a book, and he was asked why he wrote it. His answer: So that I'd have a guide to help *me* get through these ordeals about which I write. These instructions are as much for me as they are for you. Remember that I am an actor too, first and foremost, with sights set on winning an Oscar. At this very moment, I—much like you—am dealing with my very own problems and worries. So while this book may offend some readers, and while it certainly will criticize, it is necessary. While some may disagree with some of what I have to say, I charge forward nonetheless. While some may be appalled, I take back nothing. While some may vilify my political incorrectness, I care in the least. These critics are of no concern to me.

I have but one concern: to motivate actors and artists to get off their butts, and go make it happen. I'm not out to appease the media, to suck up to agents, to make friends, or for that matter, even to make enemies. I have one goal, and that is to inspire you, the artist. I cannot accomplish that goal if I am subtle, misleading, and nurturing. I am *not* your safety net. I am your kick in the pants. I will not beat around the bush.

So take a deep breath, grab that highlighter, and start reading. Then, kick your gears into overdrive and start kicking some major theatrical butt!

Contents

It's now time for me to show you how fun and easy it truly is to succeed in this business if you simply put your mind to it. Attitude, positive attitude...*that* is the key, and that is what I aim to instill within you. Prepare yourself. Prepare to be inspired like never before.

PART A:
PSYCHOLOGY

This business is, without a doubt, among the toughest in the world in which to survive and succeed. There can be no denying that becoming a successful actor is near to impossible... but so was putting a man on the moon. With the right attitude, absolutely anything is possible. There is no reason in the world to explain why you can't become a successful self-supporting thespian. In the big thick of things, it's not *that* hard. People have done it before, and so will you. Truly, zenly speaking, becoming a successful actor is absurdly *easy*, as long as you are willing to work extremely *hard*.

CHAPTER ONE:
ATTITUDE

A) MAKE IT HAPPEN

Rise and shine folks! Smell the coffee! Get out of bed! Here's a wakeup call courtesy of Unstoppable Artists Business School: GET OFF YOUR BUTT AND MAKE IT HAPPEN! There is no try. There is either do, or don't do.

Get it? It's time to put things in overdrive. If you want it, go out there and get it! There is nothing in your way. The only thing stopping you is yourself! It's time to stop dilly-dallying. It's time to get on the ball and make it happen.

Now I know some of you are already thinking, "That's his advice? Go and make it happen. I just bought this book to hear *that*? It's just not that easy."

My fellow actors, it IS that easy. Succeeding as an actor is *incredibly* easy if you are willing to work *incredibly* hard.

Your success will come down to one often-overlooked aspect: Attitude. Attitude is the reason the majority of successful actors succeed, and why the majority of failures… fail. Over 99% of 'actors' quit within their first year of pursuit. Most of these people were probably talented, had much going for them, and might have made it… if they had the right attitude, made a vow to succeed, and didn't back down.

If you've got the attitude, you've got it all. Attitude is everything. A positive attitude will be an essential key to your success.

In this business, though, I'll go a step further and say that one needs more than a positive attitude. One needs to have a 100% confident "I am among the best actors in the world, and nothing is going to get in my way" attitude. If you don't think you have a chance... I assure you, you don't.

If you want to succeed in this business where the supply for actors is high and the demand is low, you better get any trace of negativity or pessimism out of your system from the outset. If you don't think you are as good as any other actor already out there on stage, film, or TV, you are already relegating yourself to the rear. If you don't think you are just as good, and just as worthy of success, as the stars, then you are doing yourself a grave disservice.

If such is the case, you are essentially saying to everyone you meet, "Don't waste your time with me, because I'm not worth it." If you don't think you are better than Joe Schmo is, then it will come across that way, and Joe Schmo will end up looking better than you... and getting the role.

Never for a moment think, "I'm just an OK actor". Hello! Who wants to hire an 'OK' actor? No one! From this moment on, you had better start thinking to yourself during all waking hours that you are the *best*. Say out loud: I am the best actor on the face of this planet! Plaster it across your walls, on your ceiling, in your car! (This does *not* mean best person... but that's stuff for other books!)

Truly, if you don't think you can win an Oscar, a Tony, *and* a SAG award, you won't win anything. With such a poor attitude, you have already lost, because somebody else out there thinks he *can* win, and he is going to smash you into the ground.

To simply be a competitor in this business, you need to think positively, and believe that you are indeed the next big thing. Otherwise... you have already lost.

B) AM GOING

Therefore, don't make wishy-washy goals lacking in confidence and direction. Don't say, "I hope to succeed," or "I wish I were a Broadway star," or "I would like to win an Oscar." Have some guts and say, "I am *going* to succeed," because you will. Say, "I am *going* to be a Broadway star," because you are. Say, "I am *going* to win that Oscar," because it's true.

Whenever you make goals for yourself, start them with the words, I AM GOING. By doing so, you give yourself accountability, and moreover, confidence. Say it out loud, and scream it: I AM GOING TO SUCCEED! Feels good, doesn't it?

Enough with the dreams. You no longer have dreams, only realities in the making.

You have to be positive! It's all going to happen, and you are going to succeed. Oh yes, oh yes. You can not think for even a moment that you are second class and are going to fail. You are first class, A-class, number one, the best, and you are going to succeed, make it, do it! Everything is going to happen exactly as you plan it! Don't listen to what anyone else tells you, and don't rely on someone else to give you encouragement!

You have to believe in yourself. *You* have to believe that you are going to succeed. *You* have to believe that you are going to be on the next cover of *People Magazine*… because you will be, right?

If you aren't in front of that mirror practicing that Oscar speech, or on the couch, practicing that interview with Leno, Conan, and Letterman, then you had better start. Is this insanity? No, it's confidence that leads to success. Just don't get lost in yourself and your dreams; continually get back to the hard work that is going to make those dreams a reality. If you can already see yourself succeeding, then you will already have a better chance of doing so.

C) THE FUTURE IS YOURS

Say to yourself, "I already know I am going to succeed. There is nothing in my way." And really believe it. Really understand what it means. Think about it for a moment.

If you already know you are going to succeed, is there anything in your way? If you already know you are going to succeed, should you worry when an obstacle crosses your path? No! If you already know that you are going to succeed, when you come across a 'roadblock', all that it will mean is that you weren't meant to succeed through *that* path.

What this means is that the future is truly of your creation. Picture yourself in your living room with an Oscar on your mantle ten years from now. That is *your* Oscar! Congratulations. You did it! You won an Oscar! Go ahead, smile!

Now, since it is foretold that you will win an Oscar, does it matter that you are going through rough times now? Does it matter that *this* agent doesn't want to sign with you? Does it matter that *that* casting director said you're a bad actor? No, No, and No! Will anything get in your way? Not at all, because in the end, you win the Oscar!

Think about that. If you already know, for a fact, that in the end you win, is *anything* really in your way? Are there any obstacles *truly* impeding you? No way!

If you know that you win in the end, it must logically follow that ultimately you don't lose along the way. You may run into temporary setbacks, but obviously, they won't impede you for long, because you have already seen into the future... and in the future, it is foretold, you win that Oscar.

If you truly believe that your success is foretold, then there are no longer any obstacles in your path. You no longer have unwieldy problems, but rather delicious challenges. You no longer have obstacles, but rather temporary roadblocks that you will somehow weave around. If you *know* that you make it in the end, then it follows that you *must* have somehow found a way around every roadblock you encounter.

The only way you will be creative enough to overcome obstacles is by wanting—*absolutely needing*—to succeed. More than anything. You really do need to want it more than anything. You need to be completely and totally obsessed with success. When you finally become resolved to succeed like no one has ever done before, your determination will act as a pathfinder and bulldozer in creating avenues of opportunity.

If you are not dedicated to your pursuit, and not determined to make it at all costs, then when an obstacle crosses your path, you will try to avoid it, rather than embrace it and use it to your advantage.

D) AIM HIGH AND ADD PRESSURE

But I don't want to win an Oscar you say. I don't even want to be a big star. I don't want to make millions of dollars as an actor. I don't have great ambition.

But, don't you see, there are others who do, and they are your competition. They will end up working harder than you, simply because winning an Oscar and becoming a star is that much harder to achieve. Don't lose sight of the fact that there are those out there who aim to win *multiple* Oscars. How much harder do you think they are going to work than he who *just* wants to be a lead in one studio film?

Put pressure on yourself. If you give yourself forever to accomplish something, you are giving yourself room to fail. You do not want breathing room. You want to put so much pressure on yourself that you feel the only way you will be able to succeed is if you work 80-hour weeks, never sleep, and forget to eat. Sometimes I do just that.

In other words, set your sights high, and have a short timeframe. I call it TTT, or Times Two & Tomorrow. Whatever your true objective and timeline is…multiply times two & tomorrow. Aim higher than you want to go and put some anxiety-creating time pressure on yourself. While you may want nothing more than to *just* become a 'working actor' in the next 15 years, if you even want to have a chance, you had better be fighting for that Oscar, and in three years. If you *simply* want to be on a sitcom, you had better be fighting to *star* in a sitcom, and soon. If you *simply* want to be on Broadway, even in just a few shows, just to have a chance, you had better set your sights higher, and be fighting to win that Tony award, this year. And if you want to win just *one* measly Oscar… you had better be fighting to win ten, and now.

So be confident, be proud, be enthusiastic, and most importantly, know that you are going to succeed. Don't be surprised if some people actually start to think you are cocky and arrogant, or get the feeling that you think you are better than they are. First of all, you probably *are* better than they are. Secondly, true confidence is often perceived by the weak as arrogance and cockiness. Keep that in mind. Just because people think you are arrogant and cocky does not mean you are.

CHAPTER TWO:
UNLUCKY

A) I'M WHAT?

Guess what? There is no such thing as luck. Your success as a professional actor has *nothing* to do with *that*. Let's get this out of the way from the outset.

From this moment on, the word lucky should be erased from your vocabulary. As Teddy Roosevelt once said, "I have found that the harder someone works, the luckier he becomes." In other words, the word 'lucky' is how a lazy person describes someone who works hard. This is so important, I am going to repeat it: The word 'lucky' is how a lazy person describes someone who works hard. The only reason people fail in this (or any) business is because they are lazy and don't work hard enough. It's as simple as that.

There can be no dispute: It *is* all about being at the right place at the right time. But surprise, it is *you* who determines whether you ever have the opportunity to be in the right place at the right time. The more you do and the more active you are... the more likely you will be 'lucky' enough to be in 'the right place at the right time.'

Once you come to understand this new definition of luck, whereby success comes merely through hard work, you will begin to realize that being called 'lucky' is actually quite an insult. The 'luckier' you become in the eyes of others, the more you will realize that your success had absolutely nothing to do with luck. In other words, luck is something that is created, not something one has or does not have. This is why those actors who are considered 'lucky', somehow are *always* lucky.

B) HARD EARNED PRIDE

It's time to start taking pride in your accomplishments! Your success has nothing to do with luck! Isn't that a wonderful thing to know? Is it not liberating to know that luck will not ever be a determining factor in your success?

While you may owe much gratitude to God, I will say again that your success, my success, or anyone's success, owes absolutely nothing to luck. Luck does not, and will never enter the equation, as hard work is the true determinant of success.

It is truly disheartening when meeting some struggling actor who has been fruitlessly trying for years to get an agent, a manager, a union card, or an audition say how really lucky other actors are to have those things. They don't realize that the reason they themselves don't have those very same things is directly related to their own poor attitude.

They don't realize that the 'lucky' ones actually worked *really* hard to achieve most of these things. It is unfortunate that they don't realize that what they really want to say is, "Wow, I wish I worked as hard as she did! Maybe then I would have actually accomplished something."

C) NO EXCUSE

So stop calling other people lucky, and stop making excuses. As my Drill Sergeant at Ft. Benning used to tell me, "Suck it up, and drive on, Private!"

An excuse is simply a way for a lazy person to feel better. There are no excuses. If you end up not accomplishing something, it's because you really didn't want it in the first place. That is the truth.

If there is something you absolutely would literally die without having... somehow you would figure out how to get it... or you would die. If you give up the pursuit of something, or if for some reason you don't achieve what you set out to do, it's because deep down, it wasn't really all that important to you. Whether if be the demands of another job, sacrifices for family, or simply a loss of interest… if you do not follow through and achieve something, it's because it wasn't that important to you to begin with.

We give up our pursuit of something when we realize it isn't that important to us, whether it be an award, a job, a girl, a guy, or a mission. If you are serious about getting something, there is no excuse why you gave up and failed. Remember: you haven't failed until you've given up, and you haven't given up as long as you are earnestly trying.

D) BLAME YOURSELF

From this moment on, you will stop making excuses for why this or that didn't happen. From now on, your new response is, "I failed because I didn't try hard enough." This is the only reason you don't get what you want, in this business, any business, or in any walk of life. Failure is of self-creation, just as success is within anyone's reach.

You cannot blame your agent, you cannot blame your manager, you cannot blame the industry, you cannot blame your talent or looks, you cannot blame your age, you cannot blame your sex or race, and you cannot blame your fellow actors. The blame falls only on you.

There is no need to make excuses. You are winning that stinkin' Oscar or Tony, you are going to star on a sitcom, and you are going to produce your own films… and there will be no more talk about it!

So stop making excuses and start making progress. You are your own biggest obstacle. Nay, you are your *only* obstacle. The only thing standing between you and success is yourself.

E) BREAK DIVING™

Actors are always heard complaining: I just need a break! Well guess what? They're right in front of you, even though you may not see them immediately. You see, most breaks are veiled as obstacles, and are hidden in a shroud of excuses. You cannot expect breaks to fall at your feet. You have to find them

You say you just *need* a break; I say you just need to *find* a break. You have to take what you are given, and make it the break that you're looking for. Try this: next time an obstacle comes your way, think of it as a veiled break, a break in disguise, and continue to push for success even when it would seem logical to quit. You will likely surprise yourself.

Go out there, and find and make your *own* opportunities. If they aren't jumping right out at you... then you should be diving in and searching for *them*. I call it 'break diving'. If there are no parts for you (so you think), then get off your butt and make them appear on your own terms. Do *something*. Don't just sit around, complain, and make excuses.

Excuses are the gods of losers and quitters. It's easy to come up with an excuse. It's a cowardly way to rationalize failure. It helps you feel better about yourself because an excuse *always* allows you to put the blame on someone or something else. Truly, who wants to admit that they failed because of *their* ineptitude and laziness? Not me!

Yet, you must acknowledge that your failure is of self-creation. You must take accountability for all you accomplish, and all you do not accomplish. There is no luck, and there can be no excuses.

Ask an actor why he has no representation, why he is not in the unions, and why he is not being read for principal roles, and ten-to-one, he's got some excuse. I could start to list them, but there are far too many to even begin to do so.

As I know from my military affiliations, when asked why something didn't go as planned, the correct answer is, "NO EXCUSE, SIR." One is expected to complete the mission despite the situation. This should be your mentality too. If you don't go out there and crush your competition, your competition is going to crush you.

Memorize the Break Diver's Creed: *No Rules. No Excuses. No Regrets.* If you are interested, you may apply for membership in the American Break Diving Association at www.BreakDiving.com.

F) ACCOUNTABILITY

Next time someone asks you why you aren't in the unions... the answer is, "There is no excuse. I should be working harder." Next time someone wonders why you don't have an agent, your response should be, "I have no excuse. I should be working harder." When you ask yourself why you are never brought in to read for principal roles (as you surely will), guess what the answer is? That's right, the answer is, "I have no excuse. I should be working harder."

I am so tired of hearing others being called lucky because of what they have accomplished through hard work. I am also equally tired of hearing from the same mouths the lame excuses why they just aren't making progress.

According to many, the only reason I am succeeding as an actor is
-because (unlike them) I live rent-free (at my folks' place)
-because (unlike them) I *know* people
-because (unlike them) I once interned at a casting office
-because (unlike them) I have credits
-because (unlike them) I am in SAG
-because (unlike them) I am not a 'minority'
-because (unlike them) I am a guy
-because (unlike them) I am young

Man, oh, man, the excuses fly at me from every direction. STOP WITH THE DAMNED EXCUSES!

So, you are older than I am. Is that it? You've given up? So you're not in the unions. Why not? Is this your excuse why you aren't succeeding? Is that going to be your excuse ten years from now when you are still struggling?

So, big deal, you don't know people and don't have any credits. Guess what? Six years ago *I* knew no one and had no credits, too! But I've been working my butt off these last six years, and my situation has changed dramatically.

Six years ago [two years in the first edition] I knew nothing about the acting business... and now I'm a professional actor, I've started my own film production company, I've started my own band, I've started a company to help other artists succeed, and have written a number of books on the subject to inspire them. Is that luck? No, that's admirable, and it took nothing more than a lot of hard work.

Never forget: There are some actors that watch the Oscars and Tonys... and then there are those actors who go out and win them. Luck is created. Luck is created. Luck is created.

If you really want to accomplish something, you most certainly will, *one way or another.*

CHAPTER THREE:
WALL STREET

A) THE ACTOR'S MBA

Let's get first things first: You are *not* an actor; you a businessman, plain and simple. Forget what anyone tells you about your pursuit of acting being an art. It is not an art… until you are on the set. Even then, being on set is just *another* business opportunity; an opportunity to sell your services once again to the cast and crew to help beget other jobs.

As far as Unstoppable Artists Business School is concerned, an MBA (Master of Business Administration) is far more relevant to an acting career than an MFA (Master of Fine Arts), and for one reason. As an actor, you are running a business, not a talent show. There is now even something called a ME, or Master of Entrepreneurship. Now *that* is a degree that might actually help you make some money as an actor! (And yes, I am currently at Pace University's Lubin School of Business and Western Carolina University studying towards both of those degrees.)

If you want to teach acting, then get your years of artistic & theatrical education. If you want to act as a profession, get out there and do it, and be sure you know how to conduct business…real business, seriously.

I'll say it again: *BUSINESS*. You will not succeed by learning the 'Business of Being an Actor', by thinking of 'Acting as a Business', or by 'Applying Business Principles to Acting", as so many classes are named. You will only succeed by learning how to conduct business… point blank. It's not about headshots, and mailings, and showcases. While that all may be a part of it, it is the *least* important part of it all.

It's about moving, never stopping, marketing, charming, and yes, schmoozing, and a never-quit attitude that blows people away. About marketing, advertising, publicity, sales, networking, financial planning, fundraising, investing, negotiation, strategy, and vision. If 'mailings' [PRESS KITS!] come into that, fine, but that's *not* what it's all about. It's not the *business of acting*. It's business, cut and dry. If you don't plan on being a businessman, don't plan on making money as an actor either—let alone becoming a movie or Broadway star.

It is often said that a successful actor would likely have succeeded in any other career he may have found himself. Why is this the case? A successful actor is nothing other than the consummate MBA businessman entrepreneur with a winning no-quit attitude. Really think about that. Consider whether you consider yourself a gung-ho businessman & entrepreneur. If not… you had better start!

B) YOU, INC.

This "I'm just an actor" misconception is why most people find it difficult to get anywhere in this business. They don't put forth enough effort, because they don't consider the magnitude of what they are trying to do, which is to get a startup business off the ground and become profitable before going bankrupt.

Did you know that most entertainment accountants suggest that an actor incorporate after they begin to make over $80,000/year? Can you imagine that—Incorporating yourself? Sounds pretty arrogant for a lone actor to incorporate, doesn't it?

Friends, you are *not* incorporating yourself as an actor. You would be incorporating your *business*, which originally began as a sole-proprietorship. At this very moment, you are John Doe DBA (Doing Business As) John Doe. Don't you get it? That publicist, that agent, that photographer, and that manager… are all independent contractors. You have started your own business, they are your employees, and you are paying *them!* Eureka! You are an entrepreneur! Hint, Hint: Get a subscription to *Entrepreneur* magazine.

Additionally, you *must* read an article entitled, "The Brand Called You" in a magazine called *Fast Company*. It's a great article for actors. Why? It has nothing to do with acting. It's all about business. You can gain access to it by searching the archives on the FastCompany.com website, or in my new book, *Operation: STARDOM Book One*. Bottom line: search for this article, find it, print it, read it, and then live by it. It talks about your new business, appropriately called Me, Inc.

Everything you do from this day forward, good, bad, or indifferent, is a reflection on You, Inc. Your company's reputation is at stake with every step you take. You *must* start thinking of yourself as a business entity, a corporation, all its own...and NOW! You are NOT "selling yourself" (that's prostitution); you are selling your *business*! Even more precisely, you are selling the services that your company is offering.

So don't think of yourself as an actor, and don't think that you are selling yourself as an actor. You are a salesman, plain and simple, trying to get someone to bring his business to you rather than looking somewhere else.

Take what you are doing *very* seriously. This is serious business.

C) JUST FORGET ACTING!

Financial success in showbusiness has very little to do with acting, art, or talent. It's all about business. Yet actors spend years and hundreds of thousands of dollars learning their 'craft'. For what? So they can look back in ten years, having accomplished little, and wonder what went wrong?

Those two and four year acting schools are taking money from people who are too scared to just jump right into the reality of what showbusiness is all about: business. Sure, the schools may teach the actor more about his craft, which is important, but what good is that if he has no idea what to do with it? These schools teach next to nothing about business. Without business sense and acumen... the talented and trained actor is lost.

Talent does not preclude business training. It's the other way around. Yet most of these pretentious drama schools do not seem to realize this.

These acting schools allow scared and gutless actors to postpone the inevitable: starting their own business.

You can't be an actor if you have no guts. You don't learn in the coddled world, you learn in the competitive world. You are not an actor! You are a businessman. You are not in the business of show, as it is said. You are in business, plain and simple.

You must study marketing! You must talk to a publicist! You must strike up a relationship with an entertainment attorney! You must learn how to be a salesman! You must learn how to influence people! You must write out and form a business plan! You must start thinking like a businessman! You must start reading business books!

I find it very interesting that a mere 10% of the books most 'actors' have on their bookshelves are about business. I am not talking about books about the business of being an actor, or how to 'sell oneself' as an actor (That's prostitution, remember?). I am talking about business books, plain and simple. I'm talking about books about selling, about advertising, about marketing, about promotions, and books about profit margins, and economies of scale. I am talking about books about how to start and run a successful business.

Never forget: that *is* what you are doing. You are running a venture capital startup business with a plan to soon turn a profit. Don't forget that. Ever.

NOTE: the keyword is *soon*, i.e. get off your ass and start making it happen *right now*!

D) VENTURE CAPITAL

Acting is venture capital business at its most basic. Venture capital is money invested in a new and risky enterprise or business in hopes of making a big profit in the future. It is also known as 'risk capital' because the business has not yet proven itself.

This means that you *have* to use money you don't have in order get your business off the ground in order to pay back that money that you borrowed that you didn't have in the first place. In layman's terms: Go into debt! It's venture capital business!

Those of you who have read *Rich Dad Poor Dad* know exactly what I am talking about. Quite simply, there are two types of debt. Good debt & bad debt. Good debt is using money you don't have to buy something that is *going* to bring that money back to you. Bad debt is using money you don't have to buy something that is *never going* to come back to you.

Unless you have a never-ending supply of money, you simply *have* to spend money you don't have. You *have* to take out loans. You *have* to borrow and beg for money. You are *expected* to go into debt, and it's OK! It's OK! Smile, and take a deep breath! Going into debt when getting started with a business is fine as long as you weigh the options and make promising investments.

As Phil Town points out in his amazing (but advanced) stock market investment book, *Rule # 1*, business debt is not bad as long as the business can repay that debt within three years, and as long as it is good debt. Business debt is not some 'crazy cookiness' that I came up with on my own; it is how the millions of successful small businesses in America have been able to grow and prosper.

Keep in mind that you are not starving actors; you are venture capital businessmen. You are not an artist who has to learn business; you are an entrepreneur who happens to have a business in the arts. Are you starting to get it? You need to hustle and move and make things happen quickly before your business goes under. You have to spend lots of money in order to stay afloat until those profits start rolling in.

You cannot put off ordering new headshots because you 'don't have the money.' You cannot come to the conclusion that you must wait to buy that computer and printer because you are currently in debt. You cannot use lack of money as an excuse for why you aren't staying competitive. If you start skimping, you are losing valuable time and putting to waste all the marketing efforts in which you have already invested.

You simply cannot afford to be a stop and go actor. You have to be ON all the time, and always moving up the ladder of publicity, exposure, and improvement. If you do not spend money, and lots of it, to keep your business afloat and in the public eye, then you are failing yourself, and your business is failing too. Did you get that last point? If you don't spend money, your business is going to fail!

So find that money somehow. The easiest, and most taboo, way to keep this business of yours afloat is with... credit cards. Keep reading, folks!

It is a proven fact that 90% of successful small businesses in America were started using credit cards. And you might remember that Kevin Smith shot his first film, *Clerks*, on a $25,000 budget financed by... credit cards. He's certainly not the only one, that's for sure.

So why is this the case? The answer is simple: a loan from a bank via a credit card is a heck of a lot easier to secure than a business loan from a bank through a business plan. Why go through all the hassle of putting together a business plan and credit checks... when you don't have to? Are you starting to see how absolutely wonderful credit cards can be when used and invested wisely and prudently on *good* debt?

On that note, oh fellow entrepreneurs, I hereby authorize you to start spending. You are to charge anything to this card that will benefit your career (as long as it qualifies as good debt, and you're quite certain you'll be able to repay it within about three years). If a purchase now will help make your business competitive later, and profitable down the line, it's likely something you need. Don't worry if you can't pay it off for a while!

Just keep charging that credit card and buying the things you need. Need headshots? Charge it. Need a publicist? Charge it. Want to take a class, but don't have the money? Charge it!

When you receive an offer for a new credit card... *always* accept it, regardless of the interest rates! When it arrives, just put it in the box with all the other cards you've accepted. Then, if and when you need money to finance some well thought out business decision, you have it there, waiting for you. It blows my mind when I meet people who have 'cut up' their credit cards. WHAT?! How foolish that is! Don't cut up your credit cards. My gosh. What books are you reading? Where are you getting your financial advice? What money books have you been reading? That is the worst financial advice you could get, particularly because canceling credit cards *hurts* your credit rating because you lose part of your credit history, among other things.

Get some discipline, people! If you can't control your spending, then you are going to have quite a difficult time once your career takes off. At the very least, hold on to these extra cards and have them when you need them in an emergency.

Speaking of discipline, I do want to reiterate something: my one caution with credit cards is that you only purchase things on credit cards that you are absolutely certain are going to bring back money in return. One of the tenets of modern marketing is that you don't spend a dollar on marketing unless that marketing dollar comes back to you at least 100%.

On that note, though, if you are serious about success, and about making tons of money from acting, and you are so confident in yourself that you know it is going to happen, then what is $20,000 of debt right now? Nothing! A modest investment in your future. Sure, you certainly don't want to screw your credit rating by charging things up willy nilly—but that is exactly why I am telling you to *research first, then be impulsive.*

Just yesterday, May 31st, 2006, I charged $8,000 more on my credit card. Does it scare me? Not really. Why? Because it was a business investment in a product that is going to bring back a positive return by the end of the summer. I did my research, and then impulsively charged up $8,000 on my credit card. Yes, there is now an $8,000 liability on my financial statement, but that's only half the story. The other half of the story is that this $8,000 'blemish' is *good debt,* and is going to be gone in less than three months. In fact, it is going to be replaced by a $5000+ addition to my asset column.

Bottom line, you do have to spend money to make money. If you don't know how to manage credit card debt, and how to take out loans to finance them... you should not be an actor! If you don't know how to balance checkbooks and how to raise money, you should not be an actor. If you don't know how to RUN A BUSINESS, you should not be an actor.

My debts do not faze me one bit because I know the money is all coming back to me very shortly down the line [see chapter one]. The only debt I have is good debt. Debt for education, for marketing, for business expansion. That is it. I use credit cards, yes. I use credit card checks, too.

I also take out loans, and I borrow money. I find that money wherever I can, and I worry about paying it off later. I slowly pay it back over time as money comes in, and it *is* coming in because I made wise investments. The key is this: it is good debt that I accumulating; not bad debt.

You just gotta understand this. Debt is *not* bad if it is used to finance your startup business. Heck, the United States has a trillion-dollar national debt, yet somehow *we're* still doing pretty well! Think about that. You absolutely need to realize that your paltry five-digit debt load is not going to kill you. Really, it won't. Leveraged properly, it could very well be what determines whether ten years from now your dreams have come true, or whether your financial wariness has caused your life to become a living nightmare.

At this point, some of you may still think I'm crazy and giving bad financial advice. I have but three points for you to consider:

a) read the business books I have recommended in the appendix and learn how much money it takes for a typical startup business to take off and become profitable, and then determine whether you have even spent ¼ of that amount to date;

b) understand that the odds against an acting business are ten times more than against any other business you could have chosen. You need to spend money… lots and lots and lots of money just to remain competitive;

c) realize that the only reason people are scared to spend money they don't have is lack of self-confidence. If you knew for a fact that the money would come back to you ten times over… you would not have any qualms about spending. When fellow actors tell me they don't have money to take a class, or to get a this, or to buy a that, I shake my head in pity. These people still think they are starving actors. Poor souls.

E) FINANCIAL DELUSIONS

You can never *ever* forget that you are running a venture capital business, and that you absolutely *must* spend money that you do not have. You have to find that money somewhere.

I recommend credit cards because they are so easily accessible. Yes, the interest is quite high, but that's why they are the most accessible loans available. If you can get a loan with a lower interest rate from a bank, all the better! If you can get a grant from some organization that supports your dreams, then you're on top of the world!

Just get that money from somewhere, and do NOT be afraid to spend it. This is a risky business you have chosen for yourself… get the guts and get the glory, or get another job. Whenever you come across something that you know (not feel) will benefit your career, regardless the price, *go for it*. If you can sit back and say to yourself, "This is going to bring me money in the future above and beyond what I paid," then it makes total sense to make the investment. Notice the word, 'investment'. It is NOT debt. Debt—the bad kind—is money you don't plan to recover. Investment is money you intend to recover ten times over.

Yes, I know money is tight now. I know full well. But that is not an excuse. Lack of money is never an excuse. A personal tight money situation has never stopped me to date, and it never will. If I need something, I figure out a way to get it. So must you.

My approach isn't for everyone, but I can see with certainty that my philosophy breeds results. I teach people how to think like a businessman with no other option but to succeed.

Too many actors are looking at things backward: They believe they are a) pursuing an acting career while b) working a day job to pay the bills. They are gravely mistaken. Actually, they are a) running a startup business on one end, and b) helping to finance it through another job at the other end. You are not an artist who needs to learn business; again, you are an entrepreneur who has a business in the arts.

Don't tell people you are an actor… because you are not. Tell people you are a venture capitalist businessman… which you most certainly are! And *then* when they say, "Really?" you can say, "Yeah, I run my own business. I'm an actor." Then give them your picture business card. That's one more person who knows about You, Inc.

Further, you don't come off as some blundering fool starving actor. You come across as someone who actually might have a chance at succeeding. You come off as being serious. You come across as an Unstoppable Artist.

You come across as the venture capital businessman you are.

F) PAY YOURSELF FIRST

Oh, one last thing before we move on to the next chapter. If you have never read a book called *The Richest Man in Babylon*, I suggest you read it immediately. It talks about paying yourself first. What does that mean? It means that whenever money comes in, the first ten percent needs to go to charity, and the next ten percent needs to go to YOU—directly into an Emergency Savings Account (and any other savings accounts you have set up).

You see, the credit card companies are going to get paid. So is the phone company. So is your landlord. At the end of the month, if you have nothing left over for yourself... then you truly are a starving actor. Get over that starving mentality. If you put ten percent to charity, and ten percent into savings accounts, and *then* pay everyone else, you might be surprised to discover what happens:

  a. you are going to somehow still find the money to pay everyone else
  b. you are going to smile months later when you see how much money you have in your own name in your asset column

P.S. – Learn how to invest profitably! A handy acronym we came up with and use at the school is INVESTOR™. Commit to learning how to make money from each letter and you'll be a much happier artist, I assure you.

I – Inventions
N – Never Touch Fund (Savings)
V – Venture Capital
E – Education
S – Stock Market
T – Treasury Bills (TreasuryDirect.gov)
O – Own Business
R – Real Estate

CHAPTER FOUR:

THE RIGHT STUFF

A) PATIENCE, ENDURANCE, AND FORTITUDE

All business move in waves, from periods of elation to periods of despair. No matter how far along you may already be, there will come a time when everything just stops. Short. All of a sudden the calls stop, and the auditions stop, and it seems you are forgotten.

Let's say it again: This business moves in waves, from periods of elation to periods of despair. Let's even put it another way. In the last six months I've been happy, sad, encouraged, discouraged, devoted, fed up, on fire, then quitting, and so on, and all because of acting. What am I getting at? It's all a pendulum. It's all a wave.

Career lulls happen to EVERYONE at some point or another, even stars. Keep that in mind. During these moments, your ultimate success will depend solely on whether you stick around until things change for the better.

Right now you may be in the trough, but any day, as *always* (you'll see), you will jump back to the crest of enthusiasm. You just have to wait. You just have to hang on long enough to get back on that crest. That's the key. You must have patience. While it's true that patience doesn't pay the bills, you can never forget that you are a venture capital businessman, and that it may take time to get a solid footing.

You must expect the worst, and embrace it rationally. Success doesn't come easy in any business, especially this one, where each day that goes by hearing nothing only adds to the depression. Rest assured that success *will* happen, because you are unstoppable, but plan for the worst, nonetheless, and be patient.

You must keep up your enthusiasm even when it seems your efforts are not yielding anything positive. Keep it up! Chances are, your efforts are doing a lot for you, but the results are slow in coming. In the meantime, you *must* continue to find ways to finance your new business. You *have* to figure out a way to hang around long enough for success to take hold.

In the introduction, I mentioned that most actors quit before the first year has even past. They lacked patience. They thought it would just happen easily for them. They thought their talent would just shine right through. I am no stranger to this attitude.

When I first arrived in NY, I naively assumed that as soon as a few people saw how great I was, that I was going to get signed, and then I'd be a movie star within a couple of years. The reality turned out a little differently, but not because I wasn't good.

Performance talent alone will not mean you will make it. You need something else. Joe Contugno, director of *One Life to Live*, said to me in an acting class way back in the day, "Monroe, you are really good. Now all you need to do is stick around long enough for someone to notice!"

I translated that to mean two things: Patience (sticking around) and visibility (until someone takes notice). Does talent come into this equation at all? Nope! Talent is assumed. The key is getting your name out there and hanging in there, even when the going gets tough. The key is being patient—which actually means 'being steadfast despite opposition' if you look it up in a dictionary—and seeking to earn the three types of recognition that encompass visibility: name recognition, face recognition, and 'why' recognition. But it all starts with patience.

So, if you are among the survivors after one year pursuing acting, then give yourself a hand. You have just crossed the first hurdle (of which there are thousands, so don't get lazy! You still have to worry about the visibility, which is covered in Part B, The Tangibles.)

So continue to hang in there. If ten competitors start the race at the same time, and only one sticks around... there is no longer any competition. In this business especially, competition just withers away as time goes on. The competitors with the most endurance are the ones who are going to win. If you can hang around just a few months longer... then you'll have that much more in your favor.

Any business startup takes time to gain a reputation, to gain a loyal following, and to gain money in the form of profit. When starting any new business from scratch, it typically takes about three years before one can expect to start making a profit. Why is this? It typically takes the average business owner three years to gain the experience, the clients, and the reputation that will allow him to repay the startup costs initially invested. Now, if it takes on average three years for a 'typical' business venture to turn a profit... doesn't it make sense that an actor should give himself that much longer?

Just remember that being patient does not mean sitting around waiting for things to happen. It's a lot easier to sit on your couch and say, "I'll never quit," than it is to get out in the world and say, "I am going to make it happen." Strive for the latter. Just because you are patient does not mean that you are idle.

B) DIVERSIFICATION, VARIETY, AND OPTIONS

I have been keeping a journal of my acting adventures ever since they began six years ago (you should too), and looking back I have realized that whenever I thought of quitting, it was for only one reason. I had stopped diversifying myself. I had put all my eggs into one basket, and that one basket broke and all my eggs fell out and cracked wide open and left me with seemingly nothing left. The result: depression and a desire to quit.

So, when you send out those responses to the trades, or when you sign with that agent, or when you wrap that Feature Film, that is not the time to sit back and become idle. That is not the time to kick back and wait for a month to see if anyone calls or if anything happens. You are likely to be disappointed, think no one likes you, and then quit.

Always have another option, another possibility. Do NOT rely on one person, audition, show, film, or organization to make it happen for you. Remember that it is *your* career.

If you have only one audition this week, and that is the only thing you are doing this week to further your acting career, all your emotional eggs are in that one basket. When you don't hear from the folks at Casting, it can be devastating. Or when that one movie you're banking on gets canned by the critics, you'll be at your wits end. Or when your new agency that promised you the world dumps you, you'll become desperate.

You cannot allow depression to settle in! Once depression sets in, it begins to take over your whole life. You won't have an inclination to do ANYTHING, and you might just do the 'Q' word. I write this statement with confidence, having been there numerous times.

My advice is not to become depressed in the first place! It is miserable. Fortunately, there is a surefire way of *always* preventing depression. It's called... diversification! You must diversify! You cannot put all your eggs into the same basket just as you typically should not put all of your money into the stock of one company. If you do, when that basket (company) goes under... you will have lost it all.

My own personal theory of diversification for the arts is called 'Synergistic Diversification' which essentially means diversifying with a focus. In my case, in addition to acting, I've written books and screenplays, started a production company, started a band, etc. and have put them all under the umbrella of becoming a star. Or, all under the umbrella of my school, i.e. by giving credibility to everything I teach by practicing what I preach. Bottom line: the success of one project feeds the success of all the others. And that's a beautiful thing.

Nonetheless, even with a diversified portfolio, sometimes the market itself turns down, and money is still lost. Depression sometimes is unavoidable. But not unmanageable. As soon as you see yourself falling into depression, get out of it! Immediately! Say, "What happened is in the past! I gotta look forward. Today is the first day of the rest of my acting career!" and get out there on a new footing and kick some butt!

We all know that there is always something that you can be doing that you aren't doing now. You can always take a different class. You can always learn a different monologue. You can always try writing your cover letters differently. You can always apply for an internship at a casting firm. You can always put on your own show. You can always start your own company. You can always call a publicist. You can always write a book. You can always write a screenplay and cast yourself as the lead like good ol' Sly Stallone. (Do you laugh incredulously? That's the pitiful attitude you must rid yourself of. That is exactly how Matt Damon and Ben Affleck did it, and is incidentally exactly how I myself got hooked up with Endeavor, Creative Artists, and William Morris Agency—by *doing it myself!*)

Heck, you can always just wake up one hour earlier. The point is that you can always be doing *one more thing*. In fact, you can always be doing *TEN* more things.

When you think about quitting, ask yourself, "Have I truly been doing everything I could be doing to further my success?" If you desperately say, "Yes!" then you are mistaken.

Seek to always be doing *one more thing* towards that end you seek: acting professionally. And then... *do one more thing*. And then repeat. Constantly. More. More. Ever more! In the first edition of this book, I only recommended doing one new thing each day towards the realization of your dreams. In the last five years, though, I have realized that in my daily life, I do far more than just *one measly new thing* on my drive to the top. In fact, I am doing tens and tens of things each day on my quest for glory. When most people are content doing one simple thing (like picking up Backstage, calling an agent, or coming up with the title of a screenplay), I am only content after picking up Backstage and scouring it for every audition, calling 50 agents and getting interviews with 3, and finishing the first draft. Now *that* is something to be proud of! The key is to be doing 500 things each day on your quest to reach the top. Not just one. So do something more. Right now. Something more. Never stop! Go Go GO!

You are never doing all that you could be doing, so get out there and do something more, right now! When should you do it? Do it NOW!

C) PERSEVERENCE, STRENGTH, AND IMMOVABILITY

People will tell you to quit. People will tell you that you stink, that you're too tall, too short, too skinny, too fat, too smart, and too stupid. People will tell you that your smile is bad. People will tell you that your personality will never carry on the big screen. People will tell you that you are *too* pretty. People will tell you all sorts of horrible things. Pretty soon, all that rejection piles up and you are going to feel like the biggest piece of horse dung on the farm.

Your whole self-image will start to erode as the business begins its mission of totally destroying any confidence you may have. You are going to question your looks, and begin to realize that perhaps you aren't as good looking as you thought you were. You are going to question your talent, and begin to realize that even if you are good, there are others out there much better than you. You are going to question your importance as a person. And yes, you are going to cry.

A photographer's assistant, after looking at my proof sheets, told me not to smile, because it really looked bad. A modeling agent told me that I look like an elf. An acting agent once chuckled, and told me to my face that I was way too goofy to be considered for feature film. A casting director once burst out laughing when I started to sing a song and dance for an audition. Some guy, when I was first starting this business, told me in front of ten potential clients that I had no right to be counseling people, and that I was stealing people's money, because I myself had not yet 'made it'. It all hurts. (SCREW THEM!)

When you hear things like that over and over again… day after day, it starts to breed horrible self-doubt within you. You will start to look in the mirror and imagine things that were never there. You will start to see this thing [YOU] in the mirror that no one seems to want. You will start to think that you *are* in the wrong business. You will start to think that everyone is right. You will start to go insane. And oh yes, you will be humbled. Very humbled.

Yet, believe it or not, worst of all is what they don't tell you. When you don't get a part, or sometimes when you *do* get a part, your mind starts filling in gaps with horrible suggestions. "Oh no, they didn't like my nose!" "Oh, they picked me because I'm the short guy!" "Oh, I was never any good to begin with!"

The imagination starts running wild, planting absurd notions in your brain. Any shortcomings you subconsciously think you have will suddenly begin to surface, wreaking total havoc with your confidence and self-image. Pretty soon, you will start to believe that you *are* inferior and worthless, even though not one harsh word or comment was directed at you.

Before you know it, you will once again find yourself in a mire of despair. That inescapable and assured mire of hopelessness, self-doubt, misery, depression, and desperation that you will encounter again, and again, and again...

This is what I tell you: do not give up. Do not give up!

More importantly, do not argue with these people. Do not try to prove to them your case. Do not try to list your accomplishments or qualifications. I tried that only to find myself wasting time on someone whose mind was stubbornly fixed on the negative, and I found myself needlessly digging myself into a hole. You will *never* convince these people of anything, so don't bother. Just smile and nod.

These people are going nowhere. These people are the antithesis of all Unstoppable Artists Business School stands for, and they should be the antithesis of all you stand for too.

Do not quit, and do not argue with them! These people are morons. These people likely never pursued any of their own dreams, or if they did, gave up because they felt their goal was unattainable, or because others' made *them* feel worthless. So, now, they do the same to others who are pursuing their dreams *because they are jealous!*

They are jealous of those who are still passionately pursuing their dream, and will try to knock you down in any way they can. The key word here is jealous. They are jealous whether they acknowledge it or not. They are jealous and it is killing them to see someone else who somehow has found it within themselves to keep going regardless. They may not consciously realize what they are doing, but they are doing it nonetheless. These people are stupid. As a wise person once said, "Others' opinions of me are none of my business."

So persevere, and don't give up. Truly, if you give up on yourself, don't be surprised when others quickly follow suit and give up on you, too. Start again, and this time, double your efforts! The best time to give it your all is when you've got nothing more to give.

D) RESOLVE, TENACITY, and DETERMINATION

"The best time to give it your all is when you've got nothing more to give," I wrote in my journal one day. What does it mean? It means that when the going gets tough, the tough get going. It means that when you want to give up (You forgot to diversify!☺), that is when you will be the most resourceful and clear-headed. It's at this moment of truth when you realize that it's either all or nothing; do, or don't do; all the way, or no way at all.

Over the last six years, I have thought about quitting numerous times. Like when? Some examples that come to mind are when my band broke up for the first time, when I was sent off to Intelligence School with the Army, when I was told that I look like 'an elf' by an agent and told never ever to pursue modeling, when my key multi-million dollar investor backed out of financing my movie, or most recently, when I was deployed to Iraq for a year and a half and watched my business crumble, my band break up—a second time—and my entire life get turned upside down as I set off into a combat zone. As I would read my journal entries from all of these desperate times, I began to see a pattern: When at my wits end, there were only two decisions I gave myself. I thought about either quitting absolutely and going to law school like my dad wanted, or resolving to double my efforts and really show this town who I was. As you can surmise, I always chose the latter option. The second edition of *The Theatrical Juggernaut* that you are reading is but one of the results! But as it turns out, I very well may be getting my law degree anyway, simply because I now realize that it would certainly help me in Hollywood.

Truly, I have wanted to quit at least six or seven times just this past year, i.e. yes, *this year*. And if you say you haven't, then either you're a liar, or you are not risking enough. Anyway, in these periods of despair—absolute utter despair, I assure you—I face (yes even now) feelings that I will never get anywhere in this stupid business and that the world stinks and that I should just quit. There are only two options when in this absolutely assured mire.

When on the verge of total emotional breakdown from the harsh rejection of this business, you can only do one of two things. You can either quit, like the others before you, and say you tried, or you can resolve to kick into overdrive, double your efforts, and this time, *really* try.

The best time to give it your all is when you have nothing more to give. When they say no, you say, yes. When they say stop, you say, go.

Simply said: Do not give up when others tell you to.

I have noticed that my greatest accomplishments came soon after I decided I was not going to quit. At these moments, I always resolved that I was going to try again like never before. Suddenly, things began to happen.

E) BULL'S-EYE

You must embrace the reality that you are a juggernaut, an absolutely unstoppable force. You must grasp the notion that nothing is going to get in your way!

You *must* have tenacity to purpose. You must stray from the straight road as little as possible. You must always be looking three steps ahead. You must acknowledge that you have no alternative but to succeed. You must understand that winners never quit. You must realize that success only comes through hard work. You must recognize that all great accomplishments took *incredible* amounts of fortitude.

You must grasp and embrace the meaning of the word 'Unstoppable'. Once you do, you *will* start to hit the bull's-eye, and more consistently that you ever before imagined.

CHAPTER FIVE:
NEGATIVE EXTREMES

A) SELF-IMPORTANT PRIMA DONNAS

Too many actors start off on the right foot, actually make progress, get their foot in the door, and then suddenly find themselves out of work and incredibly confused, not to mention bitter and angry, blaming this horrible business for treating them so badly.

What's the reason? Self-importance. They become SIPID, which is my term for a self-important prima donna. For some unknown reason, there are actors out there who think they are the most important thing on the planet, yet have accomplished so little. These are the types who refuse to buy *Backstage* because they are above such amateurish conduct. These are the types who refuse to do extra work—not for any valid and well thought-out business reason—but simply because they believe themselves to be above such gutter work. These are the types who sign with agencies, and then sit back and wait for success to come to them. These are the types who are always complaining about not working, or worse, are the types who are actually doing very well, but start getting cocky, thinking that *now*, the work is just 'going to continue coming to them'. Yikes. That is suicide thinking.

And what about the signed actors that sit back and do nothing? Oy Weh! Oi Vai! What to do with these dime a dozen actors? If only they knew that their agent did not spend every waking hour working for them. If only their agents knew how little work these actors were doing to promote their business *on their own*.

Once signed, these foolish actors think that the hard work is over. They don't even realize that they've just made it one measly step higher on the ladder. Once signed, these actors stop learning about business, cancel their subscriptions to the trades, and take a vacation—ya know, because they think they deserve a victory celebration. Actors are quite prone to complacency. Moreover, actors are very prone to self-importance.

As soon as they start making some progress, they begin to lose focus, and fail to remember that success is fleeting in this business unless you keep it going. They start to think of themselves as having arrived... when, in fact, the journey has yet to even begin.

Never assume you have made it. That's the most recurring reason why most actors usually find themselves outside of the doors after they manage to weasel their way in. Not only do they stop sending thank you notes (if they ever did to begin with), but they start thinking that they deserve a break, a rest. They figure they deserve a chance to breathe, because they have finally 'made it', whatever that means. Folks, don't *ever* assume you have made it! As soon as you do, you are already on the way out. Do not get complacent!

Remember: your aim is to have *no* room for breathing. You must assume that your competition is working harder than you. You must assume that your competition is superhuman. You must assume your competition does not breathe, does not sleep, does not eat, and does not give himself breaks. You must work as hard as humanly possible if you want to even survive the first round.

You should never for a moment think that you have made it. Never. You should always be working to stay there. And move ever higher on the ladder. You should continually be reading more and more business books and trade papers, sending more and more thank you notes and press kits, creating more and more projects for yourself, and this list goes on endlessly. You need to be constantly *doing more*. You should be doing everything that you are offered, and then be learning from the experience, good or bad—unless you have a very good business reason otherwise.

In all likelihood, even when you get to the point where others actually consider you a star, and *they* think you've made it—you probably will still be struggling, trying to stay in the limelight, and keep your stardom a reality. The populace may be thinking you've made it, while you are actually in your room thinking how wrong they are!

By deciding to pursue acting, you have decided to accept the fact that you are going to have to work harder than perhaps any other individual in any other business. So don't get self-important. You are never as far as you think you are, and this is something you will have to constantly remind yourself about.

I often find myself thinking I've 'made it' after some agent calls me, or when I get some great audition, or get cast in something really cool. I feel like I'll never be struggling again. I think, "Finally, this is it!" Pretty soon, though, I realize, once again, that I am struggling. That 'awesome' opportunity that I thought was going to mean the end of the struggle turned out far less significant than hoped. No one person, talent agency, publicist, film, show, or organization is going to make it happen for you.

Success is fleeting in this business unless *you* keep up the hard work! Don't become a self-important prima donna!

Don't become SIPID. Don't act sipidly. Don't be a disgusting sipid! OK?

B) PRETEND ACTORS

On the flip side of the self-important prima donna is the pessimistic fool, AKA, the pretend actor, or the pretender.

Far too many people in this business shouldn't be in this business and are failing miserably, and are accomplishing this through no fault but their own. Far too many among us are dilettantes, dabbling in a field of dreams, with no real direction, no motivation, and a pessimistic attitude. The remaining few are Unstoppable Artists. The latter group is the only group you want to associate with, and for that matter, has any real chance.

I am willing to bet that more than half of the so-called actors in NY/LA are more aptly called pretend actors. By that I mean that most people professing to be actors are really just pretending that they are pursuing a career in show business. On the surface, it may appear that they are true thespians in hot pursuit of their dream, but delve a little into their work ethic and you will quickly see that they really do very little to further their careers.

They are so busy pretending they are actors that they have no time to actually become actors. They do so very little proactively to actually come any closer to their goals and subsequently, they are never, as it is said, in the right place at the right time. Then, of course, they wonder why. Inevitably, they become bitter, and quit, and forever curse the 'lucky' ones. As obvious as it sounds, if you sit around on the couch all day and aren't actively looking for opportunities, there is no wonder you are never in the right place at the right time.

If you weed out the majority of pretend actors (those who on the surface say that they are pursuing acting, but really don't do all that much to get where they want to go), leaving only the real actors (the ones who actually work really hard), the competition out there is really low. As far as 'making it' is concerned, the numbers are actually very good, and are most certainly in your favor… if you are an Unstoppable Artist.

Really, there isn't all that much *real* competition out there. If you are among the elite, among those who actually are working their butt off to actually make a mark for themselves, your chances are actually pretty good. If you don't give up and resolve to continue the gung-ho pursuit until you get where you want to go, you will get there. Truly, if you *really* want it… you *will* get it. I GUARANTEE that.

You have to decide which group you are in. If you aren't among the elite, you are among the common people. If you aren't in one, you are in the other. If you aren't among those that *know* they are going to succeed and who are doing *everything* within their power to reach their goals, then you are among the losers, the wannabes, the quitters, the pretenders.

If any profession is looked upon more poorly upon than acting, it's pretend acting. There is absolutely no pride in being a pretend actor. You don't want to be a pretend actor. You want to be among the actors that people respect. You want to be among the winners. You want to be an Unstoppable Artist. In this business, you're either a star… or you're starving. Which is incidently exactly how my friend Markus Leonard and I came up with the idea for 'No Ving™' back in 2002. If you don't understand what No Ving means, reread the last view sentences until you get it. ☺ Bottom line, you're either making massive amounts of money in this business…or you're not. There really is no in-between.

So make the decision today, and never look back. You will end up leaving most of your peers (and pretend actor friends) in the dust, but you will soon find yourself among other winners just like you. And being around winners promotes even more success. All right!

So don't hang around pretend actors. They want you to fail, just like them, so they won't feel so poorly about themselves. Leave them! Get away. Get far away from them, and go seek out other winners.

These pretend actors are anathema to us winners. They will do all that's in their power to drag us down. Down to the bowels of their defeat. Be wary, and stay away from them!

CHAPTER SIX:
AGAINST THE GRAIN

A) NO RULES!

There are no rules! Yahoo!

This business is the craziest in the world. You can do whatever you want, and if you do it with pizzazz, with grace, with charm, or with chutzpah, depending on the situation, you often find that you can break all the unbreakable rules, and quickly find yourself in very enviable situations.

If you want to do it, do it. Forget how others tell you it should be done, or whether it should even *be* done. Find the way that works for *you*, and DO IT. Figure out some ingenious way of getting what you want…and go get it!

In this business, there are *no* rules, and if someone tells you otherwise, they are very misled. Every day there's a new story about how someone did something differently… and succeeded. Are they shunned for breaking the rules? No, they are commended, and so you will be too. The cooler your stories about how you broke into this business… the cooler you will be. And the coolest guests on Letterman, Conan, & Leno… are those who broke the rules. How's that for incentive?

You are told to always contact agents via mail and never to call, visit, or email, that you can't have a full-time job, that you can't pursue acting if you have other priorities in life, that you need a three-minute monologue, blah blah blah… Screw that! You do what you have to do!

If you can come up with something groovy to say on the phone, call that agent!

If you can charm someone in person, stop by the office. If you think writing is your forte, send an email. That's what I did, to a whole bunch of agents, and it worked. Two responded, and the rest is history.

Heck, if you have a full-time job, and want to pursue acting part-time, and still succeed… go for it! If you have a family of ten, but still want to be a successful actor… I know you can do it, and I'm with you! And if you want to do a 30-second monologue when they insist on three minutes… do it your way, and knock 'em dead!

Remember this phrase: "Wrote and Broke." Over the last two years, I have broken, written, rewritten, and broken again the established 'rules' set forth by *someone* who thinks the road to showbiz success is straight and narrow. Phooey!

We actors are in a nasty jungle, and we're off-road ninety percent of the time. Go forth and break the rules left and right, up and down, forward and backward, and everything in between until things are happening on your terms. You *can*. You *should*. You *must*. You *will*.

Remember: the rule breakers of today are the trend setters of tomorrow.

B) CANNES 1998

Want more proof?

Cannes Film Festival, 1998. I had no invitation, and at the time, absolutely no connection at all to the entertainment industry. I was determined to get into that festival and watch some movies and meet some people if it was the last thing I did. Talk about a mission impossible.

I tried pushing my way past the guards, which didn't work. I tried sweet-talking the female with the walkie-talkie, but she kept on talking into her walkie-talkie. I tried to buy a ticket… but they were expensive, and didn't include film screenings. I was about to give up…

Then I realized something. I thought to myself, "If I'm so quick to give up right here, right now, how can I possibly expect to break into showbiz and succeed?" That's when I first put into practice my maxim: The best time to give it your all is when you have nothing more to give.

I started thinking, and thinking, and thinking... and then it came to me. An idea, a plan, that if successful, would serve to inspire me and countless others for years to come. I was going to *act* my way into Cannes. Oh yeah!

I had a snapshot of me that I had been using as a bookmark that looked (incredibly) like a headshot. I turned it over and wrote some important names on the back, and took out my American Academy of Dramatic Arts summer program card. I did some quick investigation, discovered that one of the most expensive hotels in the city was the Cannes Palace. I went to the restroom and wet my hair a bit. I then set out on a mission to succeed.

I confidently got in line where the day passes are given to press and other important people. Five people were ahead of me. I'm starting to get really nervous as I get closer and closer. The last person finished his business, was handed his pass, and moved along. Now it was my turn. Yikes. Here we go! All or nothing. *Showtime!*

I took out the picture of me and showed it briefly as I turned it over and handed her my AADA card. I started my spiel, speaking very fast, and pretending to be totally out-of-breath:

"Bonjour, Je suis tres presse! Je dois parler en Anglais. (breath, breath) OK, listen. My name is Chris Philips. I'm the star of *The Last Resort*, which is about to be screened in five minutes. I left my badge back at the Cannes Palace, and then I lost my wallet in the limo. I know this sounds stupid. The producer's name is John Macomb, and you can call him if you want. His number is right here (pointing to some names and numbers on the back of my snapshot). Miss, if I'm not there, they won't start the screening, and they're trying to sell the film, and it's going to look really bad if I'm not there, so please, you have..."

I didn't have to finish. Before I knew it, she interrupted me, "Monsieur, I don't know what you are talking about, but part of me believes you, so here's this day pass. You can have it for ten minutes. Bring it back, with the producer."

Did I bring it back? Of course not! ☺ I had the time of my life!

That afternoon, I moseyed into the American Pavilion, met some producers, and they liked my story enough that they made me an honorary producer for the week of the festival [see Appendix D].

I went back every day that week, as 20-year-old Mr. Hollywood Producer Monroe Mann... and saw every film I wanted to see. And yes, I did get to walk down the red carpeted stairs.

Yeah, baby!

C) ACTORFEST 1999

Still not convinced. How about this story:

Actorfest, New York City, 1999. An agent is giving a seminar and I was playing devil's advocate with him, and giving him a hard time. I told him that I disagreed with everything he said, and that I had far better ways of doing things. He was less than pleased.

Nonetheless, I sent him my headshot and resume because it's all about connections, right? I included a letter, continuing my barrage of fire, trying to explain my point of view.

I told him point blank that agents are not God and that they are not all that much more important than the actor. I added that I'm sure he would never have expected a letter from me. And so on. I told him he could throw my headshot in the trash once he realized who I was, or he could call me if my resume piqued his interest.

He called. "Do you have balls down to your knees or your ankles," he asked. The next day I was in his office. Kaboom.

D) UNITED STATES ARMY – 2000

When people in the industry found out that I had joined the Army National Guard while trying to pursue a career as an actor, they all pretty much laughed and scoffed at me.

"You're crazy," they said.

"You're obviously not serious about your career as an actor," they criticized.

"Then I won't work with you," said my current manager.

And so it went.

What all of them failed to realize is that my military background would—in the future—not only give me much pride and confidence in myself, but it would make others look at me in an awe-inspiring way. An actor who is in the army?! I gotta talk to this guy!

And that's exactly what has happened. Ever since joining the military, I have been brought on radio shows, interviewed on tv shows, written up in newspapers, and talked about through the grapevine… simply because I am this gung-ho actor who is also in the army.

Did I join the army for the publicity? Of course not. I did it because it was something I had to do for my country and for myself. The point, though, is that I was able to turn it to my advantage, and that it happened most certainly because I broke the rules. And breaking the rules in this case—as in most cases—has made me that much more of a cooler person.

E) THEATRICAL JUGGERNAUT - 2001

"What they heck do you know about succeeding as an actor, Monroe?!"

"Monroe, don't kid yourself. You'll never find a publisher."

"You're really unbelievable, do you know that? How can you say that you are going to write the most inspirational book for actors in the world? That's absurd."

Oh they doubted. They all doubted. Until—of course—it happened.

When I wrote the first edition of this book, I was not a hugely successful actor. Even today, as I write this second edition, I am still on my trek to the top of Hollywood. And that's what makes this book so unique. It's written—not by someone who has already done it—but by someone who is currently in the process of *doing* it. Frankly, I think there's a lot of charm in that.

Just imagine when I am on *Leno, Letterman, & Conan* in a couple of years—as a movie star—and they discover that I wrote this book years before I was a theatrical success? My gosh, talk about the cult story of the year!

What makes the story so interesting? The answer is of course: because I broke the rules.

F) LOCO DAWN FILMS – 2002

After my lovely experience in the film *Swimfan*, I vowed to find a better way to the top of show business. Coincidentally, this also coincided with the day I got so fed up with this one agent (a different one this time) that I sent him my most vitriolic letter *ever* telling him that agents aren't God, that they can't survive without actors, etc. He decided to fax that letter around to all of his casting director friends in an attempt to 'black list' me. Ooooh, I'm scared. Well, one of the casting directors was my friend at the time. Key word: was.

You see, he called me up to tell me I couldn't write letters like that. I told him I can and—well—I did. We got into a big argument and I finally told him that if I actually did get blacklisted from every casting director's office in the city, I would just write my own script, that I would start a production company to produce it, and that I would play a co-starring role in it. He laughed and told me that I would never do that. Oh really?

Four years later, Loco Dawn Films is now a reality. Our first film, *In the Wake*—which I co-wrote—is the world's first wakeboarding feature film. As of this writing, agents from Endeavor and William Morris Agency already told me they love the script and want to help me package it. Executive producers are calling me nearly every week asking to be a part of it and help finance it. And Avril Lavigne & Sum41 have even already agreed to be on the soundtrack. And who is playing a co-starring role? Ding ding! You got it. You'll find his name on the front cover of this book. SHAZAM.

Lesson: No rules people! No rules! You starting to get it?

G) 853 BROADWAY – 2003

Before the war, I really wanted an office for my school and production company. A veritable New York City office. After looking and looking, I found a really great one in Union Square on Broadway that—wow of wows—did not require a six-month security deposit. Just first and last month's rent, plus current month's rent. It came to a reasonable $6000… that I didn't have. Worse, there was another person interested and I only had 48 hours to find the money if I wanted the office.

Well, after speaking with a number of real estate agents, I realized that I could not afford to rent office space in Manhattan, even my tiny office on Broadway. That is, until I went to Subway restaurant.

I was so depressed and dejected while I ate my sandwich. So low that I realized I had nothing to lose, so I—yes, this is true—just started asking people eating in the restaurant for some advice.

"Excuse me, miss. If you had to raise $6000 in 48 hours, what would you do?

"Sir, if you had to raise…"

And so it went. I must have asked about 10 people. Everyone just laughed, shook their heads in pity, or gave me some psychotic stare. I went back to my sandwich and sat down. Suddenly, some voice to my right said something. I didn't hear what he said.

"I'm sorry?"

"Friends."

"Friends what?"

"Ask your friends. Ask everyone you have ever met. If it's that important, you'll raise the money."

This man was an angel, because that night, I went home and sent out an email to my entire mailing list asking for just that help. I didn't expect much. That all changed, though, when the first paypal payment arrived… for $500. Then $50. Then $100.

48 hours later… I had office space.

Lesson: Selur On! (That's 'No Rules' backwards.)

H) QUAD STUDIOS – 2004

In January 2004, my friend Brett Duggan and I convinced Quad Studios (one of the top two recording studios in New York City) to record our band's three-song CD *on the house*, i.e. at no charge to us. The recording engineer got his studio to agree to track and mix the CD in return for a promise that we'd record a portion of the rest of the album at their studio once we got signed.

Later that winter, we persuaded another engineer at the Hit Factory (another top recording studio in New York City) to master our CD, once again, on the house. Again, as long as we made a deal to master the rest of the album at the Hit Factory, we didn't have to pay for it. All together, the services rendered came to over $20,000. We didn't pay a dime.

Here's the rub. You ready? *They never heard the music.* We pitched ourselves, our band, our music, and our future so confidently that they had no alternative but to believe us.

I asked our recording engineer one day in the studio, "You said 'yes' before you even heard us play. Why did you do that?" His response, "Any band with as much confidence on the phone as you guys is going to make it. You said the music was good, and I believed you. I was right."

HOOAH!

What's the lesson: Break the rules already!

I) IRAQ – 2005

I was mobilized for combat in Iraq on May 24th, 2004. Talk about really bad luck, right? WRONG. Going to war with the Army for my country was probably one of the best things that ever could have happened to me.

Why? Because like everything that happens to me in my life—I figure out a way to use it to my advantage. Sure, I returned from Iraq alive, in one piece, and as a combat veteran. While there, though, I also wrote a new book called *Battle Cries for the Underdog – Fightin' Words for an Extraordinary Life* (which is now also available) and I also filmed the world's first comedic documentary about the war in Iraq (which will soon become known as *Fobbits...and Other Tales from the Lighter Side of Combat.*)

Who says war is all bad? I don't. For me it was a blessing that helped my career in ways I haven't even realized yet.

Oh I forget to mention that before leaving for Iraq, on a wing and a prayer, I sent an email off to the webmaster of the Guerrilla Marketing Association. Well, long story short, while in Iraq, that email resulted in a friendship and relationship that resulted in me starting to write another new book while in the combat zone. A new book called *Guerrilla Networking*. Written with a man who I consider one of my heroes. His name... *Jay Conrad Levinson*. The world famous author of the Guerrilla Marketing series of books. And guess who is his co-author on *Guerrilla Marketing for the Arts* as well? How do you like them apples? And all from a combat zone.

Do I really need to tell you the lesson? Didn't think so.

J) GUERRILLA WARFARE & STARDOM – 200?

Bottom line: never assume you have to play by the rules.

This business is *all* about going against the grain. I have found that those that listen verbatim to what everyone tells them in this business, and subsequently act meekly, often don't get that far because they are doing what everyone else is doing. I learned this early on: It's only when I go against the grain that I seem to make a lot of progress. It's all about being different and pursuing something that everyone says can't, and shouldn't, be done—and then doing it—and having the time of your life!

This is a dog-eat-dog business. Nay, this is WAR, and you better use every and any weapon that you can get your hands on. There is fierce competition. You have to be like the rock star's groupies, and be willing to crawl threw the rat-infested air-conditioning ducts to get backstage. You have to *be* more than your competition, *know* more than your competition, and you had better *do* more than your competition.

You have to go out there armed with knowledge about how you are going to drown your competition, and you had better start making yourself stand out. NOW!

You have to kick down doors, you have to break through windows. You can't knock softly... YOU HAVE TO BLAST THROUGH WITH A WRECKING BALL! You have to be quick. You have to be decisive. You have to get the job done quickly. You have to be a guerrilla. You *must* utilize the tenets of guerrilla warfare if you want to succeed as an actor, and eventually turn a profit.

You've probably heard of it before. Guerrilla warfare is also known as unconventional tactics. Guerrillas don't charge the enemy on a battlefield like traditional soldiers would. They wait in the darkness, in small groups, and attack when the enemy least expects it. They are lightning quick, and using whatever resources they have available, accomplish the mission before the enemy has any idea what happened. Just as quickly as they arrive, they are gone, without a trace.

Those actors that employ guerrilla tactics in the acting arena, making use of every weapon available to show themselves different from the crowd, will be on a pedestal. They are far more likely to accomplish what they set out to do than those who simply do what everyone else is doing.

CHAPTER SEVEN:
'REAL' ACTORS

A) FULL TIME

There are two types of actors, as I mentioned before. Pretend actors, and real actors. You should be aiming for the latter category. These pretend actors are ones who insist on living the Bohemian lifestyle to better impress people of their 'actor' status.

I met this guy at an audition once who told me that because I was running a successful business, because I was in the military part-time with the Army National Guard, and because I was trying to write a book—which I have now done five times incidentally—I wasn't really an actor. He actually looked down on me. He told me that since I wasn't really pursuing acting 'full-time', like he was, that I was a dilettante, a dabbler. Five years later, I do find it amusing then that I—the dabbler—am now working with the top three agencies in the world in production of a film that I wrote and in which I am going to co-star. Huh, look at that!

Then, he proceeded to tell me his charming little story about how he lives on rice and beans for breakfast, lunch, and dinner, how he lives in a run down flat in Brooklyn, how he barely has any money to pay his bills, let alone get new headshots, and on and on.

Now *that's* a 'real' actor if I ever saw one. I am so not impressed. If pursuing acting 'full-time' means starving and living like a bum... then I guess he is right! I'm not pursuing acting full-time, and that's the way I want it to stay. Be a starving actor? Don't be an idiot.

This guy is the perfect example of a pretend actor. He likes the drama and prestige of telling people he's a starving actor. That's the stupidest thing I've ever heard. He has no faith in himself, or anyone else.

There is *no* reason anyone should starve in order to pursue his career dream of becoming a professional actor. If your life is miserable the entire time you are pursuing acting, for what are you living? Where is your life? That is just pitiful.

Dude, have a regular life outside of your pursuit, so that you are comfortable and happy even when those acting jobs don't come through. Many times they won't. More on this later.

B) THE CRUCIBLE

I finally understand what is meant by the expression, "Don't need the money". Heck, off the cuff, that doesn't even make much sense, now does it? What does that mean? Don't need the money.

It means that if your job stinks and if you are miserable outside of acting, every audition will become a treacherous crucible through which you hope to break free from your hellish 'day job'. You'll never book anything that way, and your pursuit of acting won't be much fun. It *should* be fun!

If your job is great, though, and if you like it just about as much as acting, then your auditions will simply be a chance to act. It will be just a fun thing to do, rather than a pressure-filled and anxiety-ridden vehicle through which you hope to escape from your 'day job'.

Which brings me to a concept I call FFF™, or F-Cubed. It stands for Fun, Flexibility, and Financial Reward. Your day job—or as I like to call it, your current source of income—needs to be all three. If it lacks any one of those Fs, you are potentially doomed. Think about it: if your current source of income is fun and flexible, but not financially rewarding... then you'll constantly be stressed about how you're going to pay the bills, buy new marketing materials, etc. If your job is fun and financially rewarding, but not flexible... then you'll never have the time to take advantage of opportunities. And if your job is flexible and financially rewarding... but not fun, then at the end of the work day, you'll be so worn out and depressed that you won't even want to do anything for your career. So finding that FFF source of income is of paramount importance.

I myself went through perhaps every job in Manhattan before finding the ultimate FFF job: my own business. Before I started my own business, I was a waiter, I drove pedicabs, I temped, I took the census, and even played guitar in the subways (which I still do), but nothing brought in the money, was flexible, *and* truly enjoyable... until I formed Unstoppable Actors, which has now become Unstoppable Artists Business School. Then everything began to fall into place.

I work when I want; I leave for auditions when I want; the amount of money I earn is up to me. The flexibility is under my command, and I actually love my job. If stardom doesn't come for another thirty years... I will still be very happy. Best part: I have no intention of ever shutting down the school. My 'day job' is a job I plan to be doing even *after* I become a star.

Bottom line: Don't be a starving actor. That really is just stupid. Take control of your destiny. Say to yourself, "No longer will I be a slave to my job just to pursue my dream." What's the point? There *is* a job out there that is made especially for you until you become a theatrical success, so why suffer in the meantime?

While every actor must live the 'starving actor' role for a little while (because it is fun... for a while) it is absolutely imperative that you find a job that you actually like doing. It took me two years to do that—through starting my own business—and only now do I really feel like I am truly in control of my acting career.

Remember this: No Ving™! Did you figure it out yet?

C) YOUR WAY

Also, the idea that unless you give up everything to become an actor, you will never make it is balderdash. It doesn't matter what your other commitments are. You can even pursue acting with a full-time job. You can even do it if you get deployed to a combat zone for a year! You can do whatever you want to do. Make it work!

Some would say that you can't pursue acting if you are also in the military, running another business, studying languages, studying to become a private investigator, an auxiliary police officer with NYPD, playing with your band, writing books, in biking competitions, attending wakeboarding camps, producing films, and hanging out with my 'Little Brother'. Well, somehow I manage to do just that.

Just because you are a busy, interesting, and well-rounded person outside of acting does not in any way mean you are any less dedicated than the person who devotes his whole life to acting. And ironically, it is often the person who *doesn't* devote his whole life to acting who ends up as the Broadway and Hollywood star. You might be wondering why this is. Glad you asked!

You see, the busier you are with other pursuits, the more dedicated you may actually find yourself *to* acting. It's called the Law of Forced Efficiency, something I have practiced naturally for years, and first actually read about recently in Brian Tracy's book *Time Power*. Since you have less time in each day to pursue acting, you will become more productive as a matter of course in all areas. You will end up using the time you *do* have more efficiently than those who are less busy.

Because of the stigma surrounding your perceived lack-of-commitment to acting, you will end up working even harder to shake off that incorrect reputation. I often find myself still up at 3 AM responding to casting notices, writing thank you notes, adding chapters to this book and countless others, developing a new screenplay, creating phone pitches for CAA & Endeavor, writing in my journal, studying languages, perfecting speeches, writing emails to students and clients, practicing guitar, writing a new monologue, researching casting directors, scouring WhoRepresents and IMDbPRO, reading business articles and business books, and creating new systems for success... even though I have to be up at 8 AM.

People said my being in the Army would conflict with my acting. Au contraire! My military training has helped me to learn to live without sleep, to allow criticism to slide off my back, to take responsibility for my actions, and "to get more done by 8AM than most people do all day." All this to the unfortunate dismay of my competition who I 'somehow' keep leaving in the dust! Hooah!

D) THE BRIGHT SIDE

Remember, there are no such things as obstacles. Use whatever you have on your slate to your advantage. Your age/sex/race/look/job/family is not a hindrance. It's actually something to use to your advantage, if you have the guts to look at it that way.

If you have something that you consider a disadvantage... try to look on the positive side. Make a list of all the good things that come out of the situation. My running a business and being in the military has been nothing but a blessing... though I could have listened to everyone and given up and agreed that they were in total conflict with an acting career.

Always look on the bright side, and make the most of every situation. If you do, you'll find that solutions begin to take the place of problems.

CHAPTER EIGHT:
STRAIGHT TO THE TOP

A) BORN

There is a notion among the public that stars didn't struggle to get where they are now. The belief is that they just somehow made it, and that their big break was easy to come by. Oh if that isn't the farthest from the truth. Few people take into consideration the years of struggle and hardship that the stars of today went through to arrive at their current status. They didn't just wake up stars.

Every star was born… by a woman… from a womb… and was once a baby with absolutely no contacts, no experience, and no idea what was in store for them. Every star had to take that first step.

The difference between stars and wannabes is that after that first step, the stars kept taking step after step after step after step until they made it. Each time they fell, they picked themselves up, and tried again.

B) THE CLUB

I once heard someone say that Hollywood/Broadway is more a club than a profession. That's hogwash.

I do understand why they say it, though. The few people who work steadily as an actor are considered to be part of a 'lucky' club.

Nonetheless, when they (Who are *they?*) continue saying that acting is a profession for the few, already it gives off a negative vibe. Already you are being told that you are going to fail. From the outset, the naysayers are on the field, telling you that you stink and are one big loser.

Do not buy this mentality. If you subscribe to this pessimistic and pitiful mentality that success in this business is only for the few, then already you are putting yourself at a disadvantage.

From this moment on, realize that becoming a member of the 'lucky' club has nothing to do with luck. It's simply a matter of hard work. Really *really* hard work, yes, but that's truly all it takes.

C) THE FEW

In other words… you can do it! There is no reason why you shouldn't be among the few! And there's no reason you should consider this business a hobby when it is within your capability to make it your profession. Some may say this is naïve thinking, but I think it is simply confidence and ambition, two qualities that many cannot claim.

Most actors have often heard the statement, "The kindest thing you do for an actor is discourage him; to get him out of the business in any way you can, because his chances of succeeding are slim." What! That is perhaps the stupidest thing I have ever heard. Not only is this statement wrong, but whoever says it is rude, insensitive, faithless, and downright pitiful, not to mention totally uninformed.

I totally disagree with this position. It is pessimism and self-defeatism at its worst. In my opinion, the kindest thing someone can do for an actor is to commend him for being a maverick and for pursuing his dream, for being courageous, and for being an individual. The kindest thing someone can do for an actor is to encourage him, prod him, push him, bug him, and do whatever is necessary to inspire this actor to succeed, and to help him to become all he knows he can be.

Too many people discredit actors who are trying. Soon after, these actors quit, having been brainwashed into thinking that it was a silly idea to begin with, an idea that was only meant to be an outlandish dream.

These actors—these poor souls—allowed their rational mind to take over.

In this business, though, being rational is not an option. You *have* to be crazy! Albert Einstein is credited with having said that no great idea was ever accepted at first. What if *he* had given up?

It all goes back to what publicist Michael Levine talks about regarding ambition versus obsession: ambition is good, but obsession is what is going to make the difference.

D) UNSTOPPABLE

Your dreams are going to come true. It *is* going to happen. Why? Because you are going to make it happen! That's why!

Truly, it's just a matter of time until you make it. You may have to chart your own course along the way, and you may have to find ingenious ways of getting around those roadblocks, but you *will* succeed in the end. Why? Because it is already foretold.

Go and find the path that you *were* supposed to travel. There are other paths out there; so find the one that you were destined to travel. If not this agent, then another. If not this play, then the next. If not this path, then the other one.

This *other* path will be the one that will take you where you want to go, to that success that you know is already assured. So go out there and *find it!* Find the path you were destined to travel. Patience and perseverance will determine whether you do. It will be this hidden path that leads you to success.

Legendary football coach Lou Holtz said, "Show me someone who has done something worthwhile, and I'll show you someone who has overcome adversity." Success never comes easily, not for anyone.

Success did *not* come easily for today's stars, nor will it for you. Only through their hard work and determination have they made their dreams of becoming a star a reality. And guess what? So can you. Have a little faith!

Who told you that you won't become a star? Who laughed when you told them you wanted to be on Broadway? Who said that you will never make it? Check this out: *someone* has to make it. Why not you? The stars of today are *not* going to be the stars of tomorrow. Somebody has to take their place. I'll say it again: Somebody has to take their place. Why not you?

Don't listen to those who say that you won't make it. That's absurd. Of course you'll make it. You are the best! You've got what it takes. You've got the attitude, the business acumen, the patience, perseverance, diversification, and the determination. You've got all the qualities of a winner.

I truly believe that if you want something badly enough, you will find a way to make it happen. You can and *will* become a star if you want. In fact, you can do whatever you want to do in this life.

If you so desire, I truly believe you can first become a movie star, then open your own business, then get published in ten languages, then work for the CIA, then become a rock star, then become President of the United States, then retire in the Caribbean, and then have a triumphant Broadway return! Groovy! Go do it! Why not? I believe it can happen, and I can't wait to see one of my readers make it come true!

Enough with the pessimistic people telling others what can't be done. From now on, every time someone tells you that you aren't going to make it, thank him. Yes, that's right. Thank him for the encouragement.

From now on, you are going to feed off of their pessimism. You are going to use that stinky attitude of theirs to encourage you to prove yourself right.

Don't try to prove them wrong. The key is to use their negativity to fuel your own desire to prove *to yourself* that you are right, which you most certainly are. Feed off that negativity. Let it inspire you! Embrace it with arms wide open! Breathe it in. Ahhhhh...

From now on, there is no such thing as an obstacle. From now on, you are a rule-breaking trendsetting trailblazing machine. From now on, you are an Unstoppable Artist. From now on, you are a Theatrical Juggernaut.

You are ready to kick some major theatrical butt! You are going to break down the doors of Hollywood and Broadway and show them exactly who you are. You are going to succeed!

You want to be a star? It's easy. Just go out there and do it already! I'm with you all the way! I know you can do it! I have total faith in your dreams, and so should you. Remember, yours is not a dream, but rather, a reality in the making.

Go make it happen. As I said, it's really easy to do as long as you are willing to work really really hard. ☺

[NOW, READ PART B AND LEARN HOW TO PUT ALL THIS PSYCHOLOGY TO GOOD USE!]

TIRED OF THE STRUGGLE? SO WERE WE.

Learn Business… Become Successful.
Our students have.

Unstoppable Artists Business School, the company that inspired this book, is the only school for artists offering you the business skills, marketing know-how, and financial savvy to complement your talents. We offer business classes, workshops, and one-on-one mentoring for the ambitious and serious artist. Join us today. Artists *need* to learn this stuff. It makes success easier. Your future really may depend on it.

We encourage you to please check out our website at UnstoppableArtists.com, to call us at 1-888-YSTARDOM (Why not!), or to send an email to info@UnstoppableArtists.com for more information.

There are artists… and then there are Unstoppable Artists. Which would you rather be? We're the kick in the pants you've been looking for!

PART B:
THE TANGIBLES

Now that you're on your way to becoming a theatrical juggernaut, it's time to learn some of the tricks of the trade that I have picked up over the years. Each chapter is essentially a 'how to' guide on some aspect of an acting career, but with the atypical Unstoppable Artists' flair. In other words: Enjoy!

CHAPTER NINE:
THE TRADES

A) TRADE 'EM UP

I write first about the trade papers because their importance is too often the most overlooked aspect in any acting career. The trades are one of your lifebloods, and are filled with career advancing opportunities.

They are *not* for amateurs; they are for professionals. Even when you are a star, you should still be reading them, because by that time, you'll probably be writing for them. You will nonetheless *still* be reading them.

I think any actor should be buying the trades every week, regardless of station, and should constantly be on the lookout for that next breakout indie sensation. Already signed with an agent and don't need the trades casting? Truly, that agent probably is not working as hard for you as you think he is. Already working steadily as an actor? It won't last forever. Think nothing worthwhile is ever listed in the trades? Michelle Rodriguez knew better, and was cast in *Girlfight* as a result. Now she is with one of the big three and has movie contracts lined up left and right, as we all know. And when my film, *In the Wake*—the world's first wakeboarding feature film—starts casting, you can be assured that any of you who want an opportunity to audition will find just that in the casting sections of the trades.

Truly, I implore you not to stop reading the trades simply because you are now signed with an agent or manager who is now sending you out like crazy. That's wonderful... but don't get too cozy.

You *must* continue to sell your services in a never-ending drive to get work on your own. You *must!* There are a lot of gem projects hidden in the trades that a) pay good money, b) are union or will allow you to gain membership, c) end up at film festivals or off-Broadway, d) become a huge hit, e) or have a director/co-star that later becomes renowned.

If all else goes bust, you will at least gain more experience, training, and credits, from which *all* actors can benefit, at any stage of their career. A week shouldn't go by without your responding to everything and anything in the trades that meets your criteria.

And when I say criteria, be careful: don't apply for something just because you can. On the other hand, don't disregard something simply because you don't immediately see its potential. You do need to have criteria—yes—but you also need to realize that the greatest opportunities are often disguised as the exact opposite.

B) SUBSCRIPTION, BABY

Now, as obvious as it may seem, in order to benefit each week from what is contained in the trades... you have to read them each week! On that note, don't waste money buying them retail at the newsstand, and don't try to 'save' money with an online subscription. Get a print subscription delivered to your front door in addition to an online subscription, and you will benefit in more ways than you may realize.

As mentioned, you'll save money off the cover price. Secondly, and more importantly, by receiving the trades in the mail each week, it will actually act as a kick in the pants (unlike an online subscription that you tend to forget you are paying for and thus don't use as frequently).

With a paid print subscription, if you've been lazy that week, and haven't even looked through *Backstage*, when that next issue arrives and you realize you still haven't even opened the previous week's issue... you are going to feel pretty lazy. Whenever it happens to me, it gets me moving really fast.

The weekly arrival of trade papers in the mail acts as a kick in the pants for other reasons as well. Just seeing the new issue in my mailbox each week reminds me of something very important.

It reminds me always that I am an actor, and that each week, people are out there taking advantage of opportunities of which I am not taking advantage. It reminds me that someone, somewhere, is staying up one hour later than I am, sending out that many more headshots. It reminds me that if I don't get moving, and start making my dreams come true for myself, on my terms, my dreams are quickly going to pass me by. It reminds me that I don't have forever to do what I need to do. It reminds me that life is temporal. As these trade papers start to pile up, it reminds me that one week is a *very* short time.

Don't worry that the latest issue is likely to arrive a few days late in your mailbox. That doesn't matter! A few days is NOT going to mean the difference between getting an audition or having your headshot tossed in the wastebasket. I used to think the same thing... until I realized through practice that most of the projects aren't typically cast for about two weeks after they are listed in the paper. Do not worry. You have plenty of time to respond. If you do miss one project for some reason, they might call you for the next one, so it's never too late to submit.

Get your headshot and resume to as many people as you can. You may not be right for this project, but you just may be right for their next one! On that note, don't keep changing your email address and phone number. That's bad mojo baby! If you do, you'll inevitably miss out on opportunities because people can't locate you.

C) DIVERSIFY

Sending out pics and resumes faithfully each week also gives you a psychological upper hand. The idea is that you will start to lose track and forget about the ones you sent out the week before. Why is this good? In this way, you will not be disappointed as easily when nothing is heard. It's all about diversification.

Send out your headshots and resumes each week with the expectation of hearing nothing. The same with auditions. Go out on auditions expecting to hear nothing, so that when you do in fact hear nothing, you aren't bummed. Do the same with your own artistic projects: have so many in the fire that you don't care as much when one of them fails (which is inevitable).

Then, just imagine the excitement when a call does come through, and you find out that you *did* receive the part, and that your projects *are* taking off! What a rush! This is simply a practical way of saying, "Hope for the best, but plan for the worst." So diversify and forget!

To further this principal, start taking acting classes as well, so that if no one responds at all, you'll at least have the acting class. Take singing lessons, dancing lessons, karate lessons, business lessons, yoga lessons, etc—whatever that would make a nice addition to your resume. Remember that every little thing counts! Whatever is going to make you seem cooler when you are on Letterman, Leno, and Conan—DO IT! Key point here: do not take classes alone and think you are 'making progress'. Don't be so delusional. Classes are a mere 1% of the things you need to be doing in order to become successful in show business. Education is key; but action is paramount.

On that note, don't dismiss the castings for crewmembers or stage managers. It's all about connections, so get them in any way you can, even if it means starting—or simultaneously working—behind the camera or backstage! Just don't get comfortable doing that work—unless it is going to further your acting career.

You may also want to consider an internship at a casting firm or an agency, or better yet, with an entertainment publicist or an ad agency that lets you get your hands dirty. If you can swing that… you just got your foot in the door, and a whole lot more. It's not that hard. Simply write letters, and follow up with a phone call. Or find some guts and just drop by! Someone will take you on. You will (Eureka!) even find such offers for internships listed in the trades. Look for them!

Do not forget, either, to scan all the advertisements that you will run across in the trades. Call, and request more information on every single business, product, or service listed. You may not need or want dance lessons now… but you should know where you will go when you *do* need them. It is the same for singing lessons, acting classes, and any products that may be offered as well. This, in fact, is one of the top reasons why I myself read the trades: to see what services are being offered, to see what types of projects others are producing/casting, and to keep tabs on my competition. So start a file, and just throw the different advertising information into this file as it arrives. You may not need to look at any of it for months, but you should have information on *every* acting-related business at arm's reach when you do. As it is said, 'luck' is simply preparation meeting opportunity. So get prepared. Prepare yourself for the future, and do not exclude any possibilities. Start researching now!

D) HANG ON

If you are just starting out, let me tell you now that you may perhaps hear nothing after sending out the first press kit. Maybe nothing after the second. Perhaps after the tenth, you'll get one call. Or maybe you'll get responses to each press kit for the first five weeks, but then nothing for the next three months. That is the nature of the beast, and it doesn't matter how great your headshot is, how amazing your cover letter is, how many people you know, or how great an actor you are. This is a business of waves.

For all your efforts, never fail to remember that it is likely going to take *a lot* of effort on your part before things start to happen. Keep up the fight, and always fight one more round.

If you continually strive to put the odds more and more in your favor by constantly improving what you have to offer, you *will* get responses eventually.

E) ELSEWHERE

Keep in mind that the trades are not limited simply to *Backstage*. There are quite a number of other trade journals you need to devour.

On the acting front, there is also *The Hollywood Reporter, Variety*, and *Ross Reports*. While few casting notices are listed therein, they are nonetheless filled with valuable information that an actor should know about.

Additionally, casting notices are now available online, and in many cases for free. Almost every day you'll receive casting notices equivalent in value to those listed elsewhere... yet many people don't take advantage of them. God only knows why not.

On the 'business' side of things, some trades you may want to consider are *PR Week, AdWeek, AdAge, Brandweek*, and *MediaWeek*. These are just a few for starters. There are certainly others that you may want to look at, so browse the newsstands. If on the surface these trades seem unlikely to help you, just remember that acting professionally has nothing to do with acting; it's *all* business. It's all publicity, marketing, and advertising (or PMA for short). So start studying! Start buying! Start subscribing! Start replying! Start succeeding!

F) BE SEEN

By the way, one easy way to improve your promotional package is by using the QuickView Mailer. Designed by a former agent, this envelope is exactly the size of an 8 x 10 and has a clear plastic window on one side. Your headshot will be seen as soon as it arrives in the door. Now, of course, this could be either a good thing... or a bad thing, depending on what you look like and what they are trying to cast, but consider this: if some casting director is casting that day, and you look the part, you just may score a role that otherwise would never have been possible. If that agent is looking for new faces, yours may be just what they're looking for. True, your headshot may simply get thrown in the trash that much sooner, but at the same time, your headshot may get thrown in the trash that much sooner... and that means they at least saw it (and that's half the battle).

Another option—and what I have been doing lately—is just sending a cover letter with my digital headshot as a thumbnail in the top left corner with my resume on the back. In this way, my 'headshot' doesn't get thrown into the 'look at later' pile; it gets opened immediately... and that is the whole idea. They don't think it is a headshot; they think it is a letter.

Another great idea is to start your own newsletter that you send out each month to your fan base, i.e. to everyone you know. Not an email newsletter: a REAL printed newsletter that—yes—costs you money. People will take you more seriously because very rarely in this age of email will anyone spend the time, effort, or money on putting together a real newsletter. Add all the agents, casting directors, and production companies you are courting to this list... and once you start sending it, don't stop. It will hurt your credibility more if you start and stop than if you didn't start sending it at all.

Bottom line, the possibilities are really endless. The key is just to be creative and be DIFFERENT!

TRICKS OF THE TRADES

1) Get subscriptions—do *not* buy them on the newsstand.
2) Read and respond to postings *every* week.
3) Respond to *anything* that catches your eye, and *everything* that doesn't as well if it might lead to something.
4) Don't disregard notices for crew.
5) Write cover letters, always, and type them... or be purposefully and creatively different. Buy a computer!
6) Send any and all submissions in Quick View mailers, regular envelopes with a twist, or use another unique method.
7) Read all advertisements, and request information from *everyone*.
8) See ONE, above.
9) See TWO, above.
10) See THREE, above.

CHAPTER TEN

GETTING AUDITIONS (i.e. SALES!)

A) WHAT IS AN AUDITION?

An audition is an opportunity for you to convince someone in a casting position that you can be trusted to not only act the part, but that you are the most well-suited person to act the part. It is—quite simply—a sales call.

When you audition, you are selling. Surprising?

So, the absolute first thing I recommend you do is go out today and buy as many books on sales as possible. And of course, it is implied that you also need to read them once you buy them. And enroll in as many courses and schools that teach sales as you can find. Hint: Unstoppable Artists Business School. For you see, if you aren't a good salesmen, you are not going to be a very successful actor.

From writing a cover letter and making some phone calls to showing up for the audition and asking for the part... it all comes down to one often overlooked factor: you are in competition with other actors and only one of you is going to get the part. Guess what? The part is going to go to the better salesmen and *not* the better actor. I know that may seem completely counter-intuitive to some of you, but until you realize that sales drives success (and not talent), your career is not going to be as successful as it could be. Got that?

B) ENDLESS POSSIBILITIES

1. THE BREAKDOWNS

Most actors have heard of the fabled breakdowns. If you haven't, ask an actor friend. Here's the deal: legally, an actor is not entitled to purchase the breakdowns for himself. However, you may find a friend who legally does have access to the breakdowns—perhaps an agent you know—who may be able to keep you in the loop on any interesting roles being cast. Can you yourself get access to the breakdowns? As you know, I believe that anything is possible. I would never advocate breaking the law, but I do know that if you want to know what roles are being cast through the breakdowns each day... where there's a will, there's a way. ☺

1. ACTORS ACCESS

For those who aren't as resourceful as others, you can gain access to a large number of actual breakdowns released to actors directly from Breakdown Services at www.ActorsAccess.com. As of this writing, sign up is free, and you submit for most postings via the internet. It costs about $4 for each submission, or if you have a Showfax subscription, it's a flat fee for the year. There is no way to send a digital cover letter with your submissions unless the casting director requests it, which I believe is its biggest shortcoming: as I mentioned, success in showbusiness is more salesmanship than showmanship. It does not have as much to do with your headshot and resume as it does with what you say in your cover letter. Nonetheless, Actors Access is a casting tool you may want to consider using.

On that note, there are a large number of other casting services online. Just do a google search and you'll find a number of them. Craigslist comes to mind. Mandy. And the list just doesn't end. Find them!

3. PRODUCTION COMPANIES

I run my own production company, so I can also speak from the other side of the fence. Truly, getting in touch with production companies directly may be one of your best strategies if you are looking to get cast in a show or film.

There is one overarching clear reason for this: by doing so, you can skip one step in the sales process, i.e. the casting director, and get right to the person who actually has final say on hiring: the producer.

How do you do find out who is producing? Simple:

a) You can pick up Ross Reports and you'll often find a list of production companies.

b) You can pick a show you want to be a part of, and do a google search to find the production company's address.

c) You can also read the trades! There is often a *what's shooting* and a *what's showing* list of films and shows, and the production company is nearly always listed.

KEY POINT ONE: producers absolutely *hate* being called by actors. Actors are just a small cog in the entire production process wheel, and you need to take great pains to ensure you don't come across as just some other stupid loser actor wasting the valuable time of a producer. Look at it in *their* terms, i.e. what's in it for them if they decide to help you? Why *should* they help you. Hint: it has nothing to do with you and your acting talent, ok? It has to do with what you can to do to help make their film or show a reality more quickly, and how you can help make it a greater success when released/opened. That usually means you can introduce them to money or connections. Can you introduce them to money or connections and help make things happen for them? That's what they care about. Who cares about your talent?! Always ask yourself: what is in it for *them!*

KEY POINT TWO: Most people seem to agree with what I wrote up above, but many then misinterpret it and start being really fake and insincere when contacting producers in an effort to be 'powerful'. For example, an actor calling up and trying to impress the producer with all of the roles he has been in, when all the roles are student films. An actor calling up and saying, "I can introduce you to a lot of people," when that is meaningless, because anyone can introduce someone to a lot of people. The question is: are they influential people or powerful people? Ahhh, there's the rub! Another common example is an actor calling up and saying, "I know a lot of publicists, or actors, or bands, etc." Who cares! What good does that do? Any producer can find these people. Again, the question is: Can you bring money to the table? Can you get the film guaranteed distribution through Miramax? Can you get Spielberg attached? Can you arrange a meeting with Keanu Reeves, Penny Marshall, and Hilary Duff? If you hope to get cast in a producer's project, you need to make it worth their while to cast you. Get it? Bottom line, the problem often is that actors call up production companies thinking they are God's Gift to Producers in their *own* mind, but end up coming across to the producer as just another stupid actor who is *trying* to sound important. Don't try to *sound* important; *be* important, and prove it through what you can offer the producers.

4. CALLING CASTING DIRECTORS & AGENTS

Get over your unwarranted fear about calling casting directors & agents. If they didn't want you to call them, why do they list their phone number in Ross Reports, huh? You can't list your phone number and address, and then write *Don't Phone/Don't Visit*. You see, that is what is called a contradiction. So what do I do? I ignore it, and call them. I ignore it, and drop by.

Why would you call or visit casting directors? Simple: to sell your services as an actor.

Why would you call or visit an agent? Simple: to HIRE someone to help you sell your services as an actor.

"A-ha!" you say, "I *knew* I didn't have to sell! I can get an agent to do it for me!"

WRONG.

Don't you understand that in order to get an agent to work for you and to ensure that the agent who works for you is a *good* agent, you are first going to have to sell that agent on how great a company you are to work with? Key word: *SELL!*

Quick tip: you are never ever *ever* going to get around becoming and being a great salesman if you hope to succeed and remain successful in the arts. Until you realize that... you have little to look forward to but continued struggle.

KEY POINT ONE: Don't think of the receptionist as someone you need to 'get through' at all costs. The receptionist is your *friend*, and your mission when calling is to get that receptionist to think these exact words, "Wow, this person is awesome. This person has got it going on. This person could use our assistance. This person is probably going to make a lot of money. Ya know what, I am going to help this person out as much as I can."

KEY POINT TWO: Calling an agency or a casting office is usually fruitless unless you can get through the receptionist. Getting through the receptionist when calling is a very easy thing to do... *if* you have a crystal clear and exciting sales pitch, delivered with cool, crisp confidence, and you get that receptionist on your side. How long does it take to come up with a crystal clear and exciting sales pitch, delivered with cool, crisp confidence that gets the receptionist on your side? For me, it took seven years.

Want to know what the successful pitch was that I used to get through when calling acting agents?

"Hi, my name is Monroe Mann, with Loco Dawn Films. Endeavor, Creative Artists, and Willliam Morris are going crazy over a script I wrote in which I co-star. The reason I am calling you is that I'm a SAG actor with no representation as an actor, and the last thing I want to do is get kicked off my own film. I am hoping you guys may be able to help me out by representing me."

Voila. I was transferred through to the decision makers at over 16 New York agencies with grand success. I used the same pitch when calling casting directors, except I changed the last sentence to read, "I am hoping you guys may be able to help me out by bringing me in to audition for a role."

What did I use to get those larger agencies on board in the first place? I called Endeavor and pitched my script. I pitched it well enough that they requested it. They read it, and loved it. I used that momentum to get all of the other big agencies interested as well. ☺ Notice this: yes, the script was great. The 'talent' was there. But it was my attitude, sales skills, and business savvy that made things happen for me. As I have said from day one: Talent is assumed. It's your attitude and business sense that are going to make the difference.

5. TAKING OUT AN AD

Whoah! First I talk about becoming a salesman, and now I am telling you to take out an ad? Yes. Why not? Think about it. The only reason you are not being cast as often as you would like is because not enough people know about you. Because you are not a 'bankable' name yet. Therefore, doesn't it make sense that you might want to consider advertising your business a bit more? Perhaps a full-page ad in *Backstage*, or an 1/8 page ad in *Premiere*. Think that's crazy? I actually did take out a 1/8 page color ad in *Premiere*, once every other issue for a year, while I was in Iraq. The result: a larger fan-base, a number of phone calls from people who wanted to help my film, one phone call from someone who wanted to cast me in her film, and the re-enforced knowledge that advertising—when done properly—can work wonders for your bottom line.

Want more auditions? Advertise that you are an actor for hire! Come on, this isn't brain surgery. You might even do a radio commercial, or even a tv commercial. No joke! Or maybe take out an ad with a headline, "FOR SALE!" with your name underneath and a description of what acting you are capable of doing and why someone should hire you (though that headline might be crossing the line into prostitution, and I am not a big advocate of that, as I mentioned).

Look: Take an effective ad out in *Backstage, Premiere, Hollywood Reporter, Entertainment Weekly*, etc. and you very well find yourself with more auditions than you know what to do with. Every once in a while,

Backstage offers to do this for you by putting you on a page with a bunch of other actors. Go for it. If you've got something others want, you *will* get calls. I have listed myself in that section many times, and have received calls, and I have also found many actors for my own films after they advertised in that section. Think about it.

C) GIMMICKS

Just a quick notes on gimmicks: don't use them unless doing so makes you look charming and clever. Most gimmicks are a result of people refusing to take the time to figure out how to be charming and clever, so instead, they resort to doing stupid, lame, annoying, or scary things in a flawed effort to gain attention. Trust me, you don't want this kind of attention (read: WACKO). Stay strong: if you want to gain positive attention, take the time to come up with something clever and charming... even if it takes you (like me) seven years of really hard work writing a script, starting a production company, and gaining the attention of three of the top agencies in Hollywood.

CHAPTER ELEVEN:
PUBLICITY, MARKETING, & ADVERTISING

A) VISIBILITY

In show business, the whole idea is to be seen. Visibility is *numero uno* when it comes to marketing. Visibility as I define it means having THREE different types of recognition: *Name, Face, & Why* recognition. The more of each you have, the more power you are going to be able to yield in all fields.

Are you doing *everything* you can possibly do to make yourself more visible? Come on now... are you, really? Have you been writing your own press releases and sending them to the papers? Have you been standing out in front of the morning shows with your website listed on poster board? Heck, do you even have a website? Are you making that luck, or are the 'lucky' ones making you more and more envious?

I know that every once in a while *Backstage* offers to put your headshot in an issue for a fee. Why do only perhaps twenty actors do so? Here is a chance to have your headshot seen by hundreds of people... and you turn this down? I'm sure many of you, for various reasons, consider it embarrassing to list your headshot there. Why? What is embarrassing about using every marketing tool you can find? It sure isn't embarrassing when people call me for jobs!

You want to be seen as much and as often as possible. Put your ego to the side. None of you are as far along as you think you are. You want publicity whenever, and wherever, and as often as you can get it.

Consider all these people on reality television shows. *Almost every single one of them has agents and Hollywood magnates banging down their doors.* Are they giving us incredibly dramatic acting, or are they just ON TELEVISION, letting millions know more and more about them every day?

If you guessed the latter, you are right! They are being *seen*, the public is growing fond of them, and they are become a name. That's the key. If people know who you are… then already you're one up on the competition.

Quick tip: if you are in a show, you better use your bio in the program as an advertising vehicle. It sickens me when I see what some people write about. They write about how blessed they are to be in the show. How great it is to be working with this director and this cast. How this is their dream role. They write about everything they've done, instead of *what they are going to do.* They rarely list their websites (probably because they don't have one). They don't thank their fans, and worse, don't tell their fans what to do. In fact, I imagine that most of them don't even realize that the very people they are writing for are potential fans.

Come on people! BRAG! Wake up. Stop thinking like an artist; start thinking like the entrepreneur you are, and if you are given an opportunity to share your business vision and ambition with the rest of the world… USE IT. My website URL is www.FutureOscarWinner.com. I can put just my name, and that website, and those two things alone will tell anyone who reads that I am funny, charming, and ambitious… which is more than what most actors telegraph in an entire bio in a program. Not cool.

You can also check out www.WhatIsMonroeDoingThisWeek.com and again, that URL alone packs quite a marketing punch: you know that I am a mover and shaker, that my life is changing frequently, and that I am obviously doing cool things.

Don't be afraid to brag—it's the only way anyone is going to be able to realize that they can help you.

B) MARKETING ANGLE & MARKETING PLAN

Although success in business—as a rule—is primarily and irrefutably about making a sale, a large part of making that sale is marketing. And in many ways, sales is actually a subset of marketing. So before you can ever hope to make a sale, you must first have a clear understanding of marketing and particularly, how to effectively use it to enhance your business success.

To begin with, you must understand that any marketing strategy consists of two parts: your marketing angle and your marketing plan—both of which are largely ignored by most actors. Take careful note as you read this next sentence. Your marketing angle is: "Why you are different" and your marketing plan is: "*How you tell people* why you are different". Of the two, your marketing angle is infinitely more important.

You see, in order to succeed, you must spend 90% of your time determining why you are different, and spend only the remaining 10% telling people. What regretfully happens in most cases though is that most entrepreneurs—and yes that includes most actors—spend 10% of their time on their marketing angle, and end up spending 90% of their time *telling people why they are __not__ different*. Makes you reconsider everything you've been doing, doesn't it? Take a moment and ask yourself these questions: Are you foolishly spending your valuable time and money telling people that you are boring, unremarkable, and not a business worth investing in; or are you wisely telling everyone you know and meet that you are different, special, and worth investing in?

C) "P.R."

Your marketing plan—as we discussed above—is how you *tell* people why you are different. It is how you put your marketing angle out into the world, and is an integral part of your overall marketing strategy.

When you boil everything down to its root, there are only two ways that you can tell people how you are different. Pay attention. Those two ways are advertising and publicity. That's it. And despite what people try to tell you, P.R. doesn't mean public relations; first and foremost, it means that perception is more important than reality. That's what the letters P.R. *really* stand for, and should be the underlying focus of any marketing plan.

As publicist Michael Levine states in his book, *Guerrilla P.R.*, "If you package a bracelet in a Tiffany box, it will have a higher perceived value than if packaged in a K Mart box. Same bracelet, different perception."

If people *think* you are a hot commodity, even though you aren't, you are doing exactly what you are supposed to be doing. That's why even bad publicity is good (even though don't want it). If you're in the news, it follows that you are newsworthy, and therefore, that you *must* be someone important.

Therefore, I will take publicity any way I can... even if it is less than positive... and for the simply reason of exposure. If a show I am in gets canned, and so do I... AWESOME! If I'm in the news... I am important! It means more people know the name Monroe Mann.

Lesson learned? Do *whatever* you can think of to make yourself visible, whether it be doing standup, performing in the subways, taking out advertisements in newspapers, starting your own business, paying for a radio spot, writing a book, writing a press release, directing a play, getting it reviewed, or even getting *arrested*! Seriously, if you can get arrested and have it be connected in some way to your career in the arts... it is still publicity! While of course I don't advocate getting arrested, the point is that publicity is publicity is publicity is publicity. Perception is more important than reality: if people are taking interest in you, you must be someone important and special.

In other words, you can never let them forget about you. 'Perform' as often as you can in front of an audience. ANY audience. DO IT! Get your name and face out there, everywhere, anywhere, using whatever means you can! Find some ingenious way of making yourself *truly* memorable (in a good way, of course).

If you are heading for the big time... you have to be in that star mentality long before you ever arrive. You need the psyche of the star.

Part of this means looking into the future, and planning accordingly. How many of you have already been toying with the idea of advertising in *Variety* and *The Hollywood Reporter*? How many of you already have an entertainment attorney? How many of you have, like Jim Carrey did before he was a star, already written yourself a check for ten million dollars? I have, and it is hanging on my bathroom mirror and another one is in my wallet. The question is, though, do you also have a plan to make that ambition become true?

Get the ball rolling in some exciting, interesting, and unusual direction so that you stand out as more than just another actor. Do not be the typical actor whose life is devoted only to acting, and that's it. How boring! No one wants to read about this person. No one wants to be friends with this person.

That's why, in my opinion, most press kits sent to agents yield poor results. Who wants to deal with just another actor? You have to come across as different... in all aspects of your career. You have to come across as special. You have to come across as someone who has the psyche of a star. You have to come across as an Unstoppable Artist... and this is exactly why my sales pitch on the phone—written about in a previous chapter—worked so well. Refer back to what I wrote up in that previous chapter and really analyze why it worked. Then... apply it to your own career.

D) PUBLICITY & PRESS RELEASES

You *must* learn how to write your own press releases, and who to send them to. You have to be your own publicist. You *are* your own publicist.

Are you tooting your own horn? You bet you are! Don't be ashamed. You have to get your name out in front of your audience. It's as simple as that, and it's not that hard.

Just mix acting with something else you are doing... and off you go! For example, "New York Actor Raises $10,000 for Cancer Research," or "Local Resident Graces New York City Stage." Look at that! You just got press coverage as an actor, and what did it have to do with your acting? In all honesty, not that much!

Be creative and come up with some interesting hook. Examine your life front and back, figure out what about you is interesting, mix it with acting, and start writing!

Most people don't get somewhere in this business simply on their acting talents. They get there because something else is being publicized about them, and as a result, their acting careers are positively affected. For example, a famous relative, a scandal, or some venture.

Take me, for instance, and my business. I can and have used Unstoppable Artists, this book, and a whole bunch of other 'non-acting' related things to propel myself further into the limelight. They all afford me non-theatrical avenues of publicity from which I can still make a name for myself. People may know me first as the founder of Unstoppable Artists, and as an actor second, but that's OK! They will know me, and that's half the battle. Unstoppable Artists has given me (Monroe Mann, the actor) incredible publicity and popularity... and what does it have to do with my looks or acting talent? Nothing! And yet it has opened a whole lot of doors for me that would have been closed for "Monroe Mann – Actor".

Take also my very first client, Christopher Patrick Lucas. He worked on a 'Sopranos' bus tour during the day to pay his bills. One day, a reporter was on the bus. He wrote a story about the tour. Next thing Chris knows, HBO is his publicist, he's appearing on radio talk shows, he's being interviewed on television, and he's being asked to appear in even more newspapers. Last update: he bought a house with his acting income, he's the voice on a number of video games, and he is in negotiation with one of the most famous directors in the world to co-produce a film together. Sure, other factors were also involved, but it is undeniable that his 'day job' got him incredible publicity for his acting career, even though it really didn't have anything to do with his 'acting career'. By the way: Chris, thanks for being my first client! Without you, Unstoppable Artists Business School might never have come to be. Meet ya at the Oscars my friend. ☺

I could go on and on with other client/student success stories that prove this point. You must understand that you can make a name for yourself based on something else—whatever that *something else* is, and then use that fame to your theatrical advantage.

You see, nobody cares about you, the actor. Actors are a dime a dozen. Everyone is an actor. You have to start thinking like a guerrilla, and start coming up with ingenious schemes, plans, stunts, tricks, and designs that are going to make you stand out.

It's all about P.R.—Perception over Reality. You have to be different. You have to show yourself coming from a different breed. You have to package yourself in a box from Tiffany's.

NOTE: The whole point of this section is to SCREAM IN YOUR FACE the importance of learning how to write your own press releases. If after you read this book, you don't learn how to do so… shame on you.

E) PUBLICISTS

Now, don't wait until the last minute to research a publicist that you may want to work with in the future! At this moment, now, you should already be thinking about publicists, ad agencies, entertainment attorneys, fan clubs, websites, and secretaries. The only way people succeed when opportunity knocks is by having the knowledge and preparation done ahead of time so they know what to do when the time comes.

First off, if you have no idea what different publicists cost, who are the best, and what they can do for you, how are you going to know what action to take when the right time does come? If you don't consult with a publicist now, how the heck are you going to know if you have anything worthy of national publicity?

I once asked a panel of agents when the best time for me to hire a publicist would be. They all laughed at me, and one had the gall to mockingly say, "When you've got something to publicize." It was a legitimate question, and to this day it concerns me that these are the people who are purportedly the experts who are supposed to negotiate our contracts and help move our careers forward. The problem from the beginning was that I should not have been asking an *agent* that question; I should have asked an actual publicist.

The correct answer should have been, "To help build momentum on something that has already earned a small amount of publicity through your own publicity efforts." It's been five years since that bitter, jaded, and uneducated agent laughed at me. Since then, I have had four publicists on retainer, some good who secured me great publicity, some bad who did nothing for me, and in all cases, I learned a whole heck of a lot. The big problem is that most actors aren't confident enough in themselves to understand the need to start researching publicists before the big gig hits, and to learn how to do these things themselves in the meantime. Heck, most agents aren't confident enough in their actors to understand the same need, as those that laughed at me proved. It seems most actors (and agents) think that the actor should only hire a publicist when he is cast in some high profile project, and for no other reason. I look at publicity a little differently.

I do agree that you should hire a publicist when you have something to publicize, but I also understand that you can publicize a lot more than just an acting career, as I touched on in the previous section. When you publicize *anything* you are doing, your name becomes more familiar, and your acting career will benefit indirectly from the publicity gained.

If you are serious about succeeding big-time as an actor, you are going to need a publicist to get your name out there at some point or another. You may as well get on the ball now. It is *never* too early to start researching publicists.

If you don't have a subscription to Who Represents—WhoRepresents. com—yet, I suggest you get one. It allows you to look up any 'star' and see who their agent is, who their lawyer is, who their manager is, and who their... publicist is! Pretty useful information when you want to get a star involved in one of your projects, doncha think?

So, start reading up on which publicists do what. Does this firm focus on comedians, or film actors? Or showmen in general? Check out *PR Week* online—PRWeek.com—and get a grasp on which firms are best known for what types of publicity. Do a google search for general publicity firms in your area that may be able to help you on a less expensive retainer, or even for no retainer at all. There are even some publicists who you only pay... once they secure you publicity! Groovy, eh?

It typically costs about $50 - 125 to speak with a publicist for a half-hour. Do so! Maybe *you* have something worth publicizing. They will tell you. Meet with them for their measly consultation fee and benefit from their knowledge.

Remember, though, that publicists are very expensive. You have to weigh the benefits gained against the costs incurred. If by hiring a publicist, everyone on the face of the planet knows who you are, then perhaps $1500/month really isn't that much to spend. You must consider the hiring of a publicist an investment in your future... your very wealthy future.

If a publicist can get you on television, on some show about animals, talking about your extensive parrot collection... it's certainly worth the money. More people will know who you are! They may not know you as an actor... but your name just became a lot more familiar, and that's the whole idea!

If you're slick, too, while on the air, you will find some way to throw in that you are an actor. That's being Unstoppable. You can then postcard agents and casting directors and say, "Hey, watch me on *Animal World* Thursday night!" I guarantee *that* will pique their interest! Or better yet, I would turn that into a killer sales call, and call every agent in Ross Reports to secure an interview...

If, however, the press agents tells you that they can't help you right now, fret not! If they say that they can't do anything for you, you just learned something really valuable. You just learned that you had better get *off* your butt, and start *kicking* some butt. You just learned that you had better start doing something worthy of publicity! Start a business, write a book, write a revolutionary screenplay, win an award, participate in some event, SOMETHING. Then start writing those press releases I spoke about above!

Quick Tip: If you have your own book published, publicists are usually more inclined to bring you on board. Why? A book gives credibility. So write your damn book already.

F) ADVERTISING

We spoke briefly about taking out advertisements in a previous chapter. Let me just take a moment to share with you how important this all really is.

If you recall, there are only two ways you can tell people how you are different: publicity and advertising. Notice that I didn't say publicity *or* advertising. Oh no. It is not an option whether you use one or the other. You must use both.

You might ask why... The answer is simple. Advertising gives you complete control but costs a lot of money and isn't all that credible. Publicity gives you a lot of credibility and doesn't cost you much money, but it gives you very little control. If you want to have high credibility, low cost, and high control... you cannot neglect either publicity *or* advertising. It's something I call C.C.C., or C-cubed: Cost, Credibility, & Control. If you want to benefit from C-cubed, you must use both publicity *and* advertising.

That being said, what is advertising? It's simple: anytime you pay for someone to say something nice about you, it's advertising. Don't you then realize how powerful advertising is? Sure, they always say that buying your friends is uncouth, but I disagree. That's exactly what you are doing with advertising, and it pays big dividends! You pay a newspaper a couple of hundred dollars and in return, they give you some real estate on the pages of their paper and give you a permit to build WHATEVER you want to on that plot of land. Wow. That is simply amazing, and those actors who don't take advantage of such an opportunity are truly foolish.

Moreover, I have found from personal experience (and have also read in many books to back up my theories) that those people who advertise frequently and consistently with a certain media outlet typically have an easier time getting that same media outlet to give them publicity coverage. Sure, technically, there is supposed to be a separation of church and state between the editorial and advertising departments... but there really isn't. Until those two departments are run by separate companies, the editorial and advertising departments will never be separate. So if you're hunting (or hurting) for publicity, start out by taking out a bunch of ads over a consistent period of time in a certain media outlet... and then see whether your press release gets published or if you start to receive more favorable press coverage. You might be surprised.

G) AD AGENCIES

Now, regarding advertising agencies... you already have one! I say this because if you take out ads and explain that you do your own advertising, they will give you a 15% agency discount.

Agency discount? You see, when you hire an ad agency, you do not typically pay them for the work they do; the media do. If you call up an ad agency and tell them you want to take out $10,000 worth of ads in *Backstage*, you then transfer that 15% agency discount that you were going to take... to the ad agency. In other words, you pay nothing more for the services of the ad agency. Instead of designing the ads and negotiating rates yourself, and then paying the $10,000 to *Backstage* and then asking for the 15% agency discount, you would instead let the ad agency do all that work for you (under your guidance) and pay that $10,000 to the ad agency who will ask for the 15% agency discount themselves. If this doesn't make complete and total sense to you, don't worry: just realize that in most cases, you shouldn't have to pay anything more for the services of an ad agency.

For example, I recently spoke with an ad agency to start assembly of a cable television ad campaign for the school. If I bring them on board, I don't actually pay anything additional to the ad agency out of my pocket. The ad agency would place the ads for me, and then request the 15% agency discount.

FYI, many people don't know that advertising on cable television is not all that expensive because it is not national. You are not paying the cable station that is *broadcasting*—as in network television—but rather the cable company itself. Where I live it's Time-Warner Cable. And the ad is only going to broadcast in Manhattan. But since the ads will be broadcast during a 'national' television show, i.e. *Inside the Actor's Studio* on Bravo for instance, it will have the national credibility associated with that show. The same thing applies to national magazines like *People, Time*, etc. What you are reading may *look* like a national edition, but it is usually a *regional* edition, and thus the ad rates for such an ad are a whole lot less expensive. I hope you're getting some ideas here...

In fact, I really hope you're getting some ideas because for the most part, I imagine you are going to be implementing all of the ideas yourself. You see, most ad agencies aren't going to find it all that beneficial to work with you unless you have a sizeable ad budget, for the reasons stated above. There may be some exceptions, but by and large, you are going to be doing most of your ad design and placement yourself until you have gained more experience as an ad man, and until you have enough money in your ad budget to warrant the commissioning of an ad agency. For now, just do it yourself and save that 15% for the expansion of your company.

H) NEGATIVE PRESS/SPIN CONTROL

Guess what: no matter how great you are, some people are going to think you stink. No matter how much great press you receive, others are going to give you bad press.

First, you need to learn how to just go with the flow and deal with it.

Second, you need to realize that no one ever gets bad press unless they are someone important that others want to read about.

Third, realize that bad press can often be deflected by good press. In other words, in most cases, instead of trying to deflect the bad press through damage control, you might serve your business better by simply working even harder to gain good press.

In some cases, of course, the situation is so bleak that you have no alternative but to 'make a statement' and do something about it. In such cases, you *may* be given a public forum through which to do this; in other cases, you may not. In this case, you may be forced to *advertise* your sentiments and/or explanation of the situation.

No matter what, and this is the absolute truth: if you start to notice that you are getting a lot of bad press somewhere, it probably means you are starting to succeed; it probably means the peanut galley is just doing its job. Before you jump ship and cry in pity, look around. Look around for the success that is probably associated with the bad press. For instance, for the last few years, a peanut galley has formed on my IMDb page, with the sole purpose of discrediting me, criticizing me, and... killing me. ☺ I had to actually call the FBI when they started talking about sending anthrax to me in Iraq by mail. At first, I was devastated, and it hurt so much. Thousands—yes *thousands*—of posts about why Monroe sucks, why Monroe Mann is a loser, why he is never going to succeed, blah blah blah. They began adding porn credits to my IMDb film list. They actually created a WhyWeHateMonroeMann website. This was perhaps one of the lowest points of my career to date... until I realized that on the flip side of all this, my books were starting to become more popular; I was now writing a book with Jay Conrad Levinson; my film was beginning to take shape; my school was expanding; etc. I was being criticized, yes, but it was happening because I was becoming a star. Why else would so many people I didn't know take such a huge interest in criticizing me? I was becoming a public figure... and part of that 'fame' comes the 'paparazzi' and the 'peanut galley' critics. Once that became apparent... I began to smile every time someone posted another nasty comment about me on IMDb. It meant that I was becoming more and more of a success.

So let that serve as inspiration to you: if you are *not* being criticized, it probably means you're not doing enough for anyone to care. ☺

I) VISIBILITY MAKES THE STAR

If your letters, press releases, and advertisements have something to say... phones will start to ring. If you have something to publicize... and word gets out about it... money and offers *will* start to come in. If your advertising is effectively sales-driven... then you are going to make sales. If your marketing strategy effectively explains to people why you are different and why they would benefit by hiring you and/or buying from you... then you are going to become successful, no ifs, ands, or buts about it.

Too many actors think that great acting is what makes star actors hot commodities. This is not the case. Their acting talent may give them something to publicize, but it is the *publicity, marketing, & advertising* of that talent that gets doors knocking and deals offered. It is *publicity, marketing, & advertising* that make actors hot commodities, and *not* their acting talent. It is *visibility* of that actor that makes them hot commodities, and *not* their acting talent.

Always remember that. It is visibility, and not acting, that makes the star. The businessman who attacks his pursuit of acting with a mind for publicity, marketing, & advertising will succeed. The actor who is banking merely on his talent will likely fail.

So figure out your marketing angle, start writing those press releases, and start taking out those ads... now. Tomorrow, ladies and gentlemen, may simply be too late.

Reminder: Of everything written in this chapter, the most important lesson to take away is the idea of your marketing angle. You *must* figure out why you, and all of your projects, are *different!* Being different is the key to successful marketing, and until you realize this, and embrace it, all of your publicity and advertising efforts will probably be wasted.

CHAPTER TWELVE:
EXPERIENCE

A) BOMB IT!

Regardless of how many classes claim to teach you how to get better at auditions… the only way you are really going to get better at auditions is by going on real auditions, and bombing them one after the other.

Classes are just that… classes. It's theory and not practice. You have to realize that you are going to have to flub a lot of *real* auditions before you start doing them right. Only by actually doing will you become more and more confident.

So go out there and *confidently* look forward to bombing those auditions! And… sales calls! ☺

B) CONFIDENCE

Just because you didn't get the part, doesn't mean that your audition was poor. Don't assume that you were bad simply because you didn't get the part. That's the common and easy backdoor excuse. A successful actor will book 1 out of 20 auditions.

I can't tell you how many times I've gone into an audition, knocked them dead, only to find out that I didn't get the part. What happened? I was too young, too old, too tall, too short, whatever. How do I know that I knocked them dead? They called me in for an audition, *one year later*, and told me.

There are so many times when you probably really showcased yourself as a great actor, but didn't get the part because you weren't right for it for other reasons. In fact, that's usually why you didn't get the part (or at least that's what you have to think).

If you are so confident that you are talented and that you are a great actor, then rejection should mean nothing. It should simply push you to work even harder.

Do yourself a favor and don't use your perceived lack of talent as an excuse for why you don't book jobs. It's a recipe for sure-fire disaster.

After ten such auditions that leave one feeling ever more lacking in talent, it's no wonder that so many people quit. It's irrelevant whether your talent is the true reason for your not being cast; maybe you *were* really bad, but never use that as your excuse. That is just insane. Repeat over and over: I am the BEST!

C) EVERYTHING

Get in every stupid waste-of-time piece-of-crap production you can get your hands on. Why? Because there is no such thing as a stupid waste-of-time piece-of-crap production! It's all about connections, and that podunk play just might turn into a hit. One never can tell.

It's all about meeting people. Inevitably, you will a) meet someone you want to work with in the future, or b) meet someone who you never want to work with again. Either way, you win, because now you know, and in the words of GI Joe, knowing is half the battle. Moreover, you'll be practicing and doing what you love.

My one caveat here is that you don't want to get sucked into doing too many non-paying productions 'just for experience'. At a certain point, you have to just stop doing things 'for experience'. If you don't, you risk becoming a pretend actor film junkie: you've got a thousand credits and no reputation within the industry to speak of because all the film gave you was 'experience', instead of career pushing fodder.

Now, there are many other reasons to participate in a production outside of 'experience', and those are the reasons you should consider doing a 'non-paying' role. I put 'non-paying' in quotes because you should *never* do something for no pay. You need to get *something* out of it that is tangible: tape for your reel; introduction to a new director you hear is on the rise; a guarantee—in writing—that the film is going to be submitted to film festivals; etc. Make sense?

You need to get something from everything you do—even if it is just education.

So how do you get into these shows and films? Simple: Audition! Just keep auditioning. I know it sounds like cheap advice... but that's the key! Just keep doing it!

Keep networking. Keep your ears open. Keep telling people what you are doing, and why you are different. Get the trades, and reply to everything! Even if you aren't right for one production, you'll be right for something... and they'll call you in the future. It happens. So consider submitting even if you do not think that they will call you for this show. Keep mailing. Keep doing. Get more and more credits. Never dismiss opportunities. Consider it all.

On that note, don't dismiss student films just because they are student films. They are invaluable for your training, your resume, and your reel, and it is not all that difficult to get cast in them if you put your mind to it. And as I mentioned up above, as long as you can get something tangible from it, it could very well be worth it.

First consider that it's probably much easier to get into a student film than trying to get into plays because of a film director's 'fake and make' capabilities. With a film, a director can 'fake and make' talent in the editing room, and make a less-talented actor look pretty darn good. This is not the case on stage.

Remember also that film directors are first looking for a look, rather than great 'talent'. If you've got the look... you'll probably get an audition (and yes, in answer to your question, you have the look).

However, by the same token, don't dismiss theater simply because you want to do film. First, you'll really find out if you can act by doing theater. Second, that's where you are really going to improve your skills, and build your confidence. Third, that's where reviewers are most likely to see you. Fourth, it looks really good on your resume. Fifth, it's so much fun. Sixth, listed on your resume, it shows that you have been around a while. Seventh, they show that you are capable of speaking in front of an audience. Eighth, I could go on... Besides, it looks sort of shabby to just have film credits on your resume. In my opinion, it shows that you're not truly serious about acting—just movies.

Just realize that if you keep on responding, week after week, to *all* postings in the trades and from the web; if you continually stay on the prowl and effectively disseminate your marketing angle at every juncture; and if you just flat-out refuse to come up with any excuses... you *will* get auditions, and then parts, eventually. It's simply a matter of continually putting the odds more and more in your favor.

D) ODDS

On that note, here are some ways to drastically increase your odds of getting calls, getting auditions, getting parts, and getting credits. I suggest them because they work, and I know they work because I have done them all:

- How many of you have taken your headshot personally to every film school in your area and left it in the actor file?
- How many of you have done the same at every casting agency?
- How many of you have looked into going to a film program like at New York Film Academy or Digital Film Academy... and casting yourself as the lead in your own films?
- How many of you have called *Backstage* and ordered the back issues that contain the addresses of all the off-off-Broadway theater companies in New York?
- How many of you have went a step further and submitted to all of them, and then kept in touch with them?
- How many of you own a digital video camera and practice doing commercials and monologues, and then watch yourself?
- How many of you take that digital camera and film your own movies, and add the credits to your resume?
- How many of you put on your own shows?

- How many of you have offered to help as crew on a film set (student or otherwise), in order to learn what's going on... and in order to schmooze the director into including you in his next movie?
- How many of you just drop by film schools and distribute your headshot to passing students while at the same time introducing yourself. This is a SUREFIRE way of getting calls. Don't have the balls? Better find them. Think it's lame? Your competition doesn't think so.
- How many of you have sent your headshot and resume to all the opera companies in NY, including New York City Opera and the Met, directing your mail to the casting director of supernumeraries?
- How many of you even knew that there are non-singing acting roles in operas?
- How many of you use Quick View Mailers when sending out headshots and resumes or some other creative way of getting attention?
- How many of you have your official website up and running?
- How many of you have photo business cards and distribute them to *everyone* you meet?
- How many of you have business cards that proclaim your ambition right on the cards, and publicly tell everyone what you are doing?
- How many of you have read every book available on attitude, psychology, marketing financing, fund-raising, financial management, sales, advertising, publicity, networking, and negotiation? (See reading list in Annex. Also visit www. UABSBooks.com)
- How many of you have researched voice-over acting?
- How many of you have branched out into commercial print modeling?
- How many of you have looked at acting opportunities in Toronto, Vancouver, London, and Sydney?
- And this list goes on and on and on...

Opportunities abound if you simply look for them. The ideas are limited only by your imagination. The whole idea behind it all is: MAKE IT HAPPEN. Do some research. Be creative. Put the odds in your favor.

If you can't get auditions through the regular channels… find some other way of doing it. Me? After trying the traditional auditioning route, I had to write my own screenplay and start my own production company. As a result, I am now negotiating with the top five agencies in Hollywood about my film… in which I co-star. So take the road less traveled. It will make all the difference.

CHAPTER THIRTEEN:
GETTING SIGNED & GETTING CAST

A) WHO DO THEY WORK FOR, HUH?

Casting directors work for Producers. They are not the decision makers. Agents work... *for you.* They are not the decision makers. In both cases, *they are not the decision makers!* And that knowledge should help you to change the way you look at agents and casting directors forever.

B) T.A.N.G.

Here are four quick words regarding agents and casting directors: They Are Not God. They are not the only thing standing between you and stardom.

Treat them like Gods and they will harp on the opportunity to treat you like a peon. So don't treat them like Gods! They are only agents and casting directors!

When they say don't call, CALL! When they say don't stop by, STOP BY! When they say stop, KEEP ON GOING! When they say there is no hope, SHOW THEM OTHERWISE!

Truly, if you call every agent in Ross Reports in your city—which you should, and takes less than 2.5 hours—and don't get at least three interviews, then the problem is with *your pitch*, not with you and not with them. Success in business is about salesmanship; not talent, credits, or connections. Got it?

You must remember (and never forget) three things concerning talent agents and casting directors:

a) **95% of the people contacting agents and casting directors should not be in the business.** They are either arrogant and pushy, totally void of any business skills, or just plain annoying without an ounce of charm. Keep that in mind when agents treat you coldly. Although you may be the next big thing, it is going to take *a lot* to prove it to them. Yes, like it or not, you have to prove it to them. When they say they don't want you, push on anyway. When they say you have no talent, laugh at their stupidity. When they say they aren't taking on any new clients, show them why they should! Pretend actors give up when opposition gets in the way. The Oscar and Tony award winners don't do that.

b) **Agents are YOUR employees.** You are the boss, and you are doing the hiring so to speak, even though they may have more years of experience than you do (though in many cases, they are still idiots, so please beware). Try to always remember this— that agents are your employees. Keep that in mind, and treat them accordingly: with the respect afforded to an employee, but the firmness you would expect from your own boss. They may know more than you, but when push comes to shove, you are still in charge! For you folks who understand military lingo, it's sort of like the relationship between a newly commissioned Lieutenant, and the Platoon Sergeant. The LT is in charge, but given the years of experience amassed by the Platoon Sergeant, it would be wise to give him leeway, and seriously consider his advice even though he is a lower rank. But in the end, the LT makes the final decision, as he is ultimately responsible for the platoon's success or failure.

c) **Casting directors work for the PRODUCER.** Don't let casting directors be the be all and end all. They are anything but the be all and end all. They are merely independent contractors hired by the producers to help make their job easier. Just because a casting director doesn't like you doesn't mean the producer won't. If you know you are right for the part, and you are making no headway with the casting directors... go straight to the bottom line: the producers. Don't let casting directors be the bitchy gatekeepers that keep you from a successful career in showbusiness. No offense to casting directors, of course. ☺

C) THE POWER SEAT

So stop kowtowing to agents. Stop kowtowing to casting directors. Stop kowtowing to directors, and stop kowtowing to producers. Treat everyone with respect... and that's it!

Don't spend your precious time begging agents and casting directors to come to your shows. Chances are, if you invite them, they aren't going to come. Why not?

First, your show probably sucks... or rather, that's the *perception* everyone has up front unless your marketing is absolutely amazing. The problem here though is that your marketing probably isn't amazing. In all likelihood, as Mark Stevens points out in his book of the same name, it's probably not that your show sucks, but that *Your Marketing Sucks*. It probably does. This is not a criticism: it is a fact. If it didn't suck, you would be a lot more successful now ☺

Second, why go see 10 actors for free when you can go see 20 actors at commercialized showcases, and get paid $125 for doing so? Now, I completely disagree with this 'pay to meet industry' racket that's going on lately, but that doesn't mean it doesn't exist. And it is something you have to fight and take into consideration.

Sure, you can send invitations, and all that, and if it works, cheers, but you would surely better spend your time getting publicity for your show through the writing of press releases. And then using that press to get the attention of industry.

You see, ideally, you should not be asking agents, "Will you come see me?" Agents should be calling and asking, "Can I come see you?" You want to be in the power seat.

If you call agents, asking them to come to your show, they are in the position of power. On the other hand, if they call you, *you* are in the power seat, for now they have to do all the selling.

For that reason, I usually don't invite industry to come see me anymore. I focus more on getting out there and doing so much that they call me! Instead of inviting agents and casting directors to come see me in shows, I just send out postcard after postcard, saying, "Cast in…", "Cast again in", "Rehearsing for","Performing in", blah blah blah.

I usually don't invite them. I just let them know what I'm doing, and inevitably, I am called… again and again.

If as a result of 'letting them know', they come to some show you are in, fine, but that's not the point. The point is to do so much that they start thinking, "Hey, this kid's got something! He's doing something new every two weeks! I want to meet him."

And guess what? That meeting will already be in your favor. You will have the upper hand because they want to meet *you*, and not vice-versa. They called YOU! Good job! That's the whole idea.

Truly, why would you want to meet agents on *their* terms, when you are the one doing the hiring? Wait for them to come to you, and prove to *you* that they can do something for *you*, and are serious about helping *you*. I guarantee that any agent you meet on these terms will work that much harder for you, because it is obvious that they already are making efforts, on their own, to come to *you*.

Don't get me wrong. It's OK to give agents a little bait to nibble on, to see if they bite. For instance, the other day I called nearly every agent in NY with that sales pitch from earlier in the book and it worked wonders. But notice something here: while they didn't want to meet me the moment they picked up the phone, ten seconds later—because of the clear and crisp sales pitch—they absolutely did. No matter what you do you need to convince them in ten seconds that you are different and have dollar signs written all over you.

My point here is that it's a waste to spend precious time desperately trying to grab agents and casting directors with your hands—and look like an idiot in the process—when you could simply use a fishing net— and look really good in the process. So please, for your future's sake, make a pact, right here and now, never again to humiliate and degrade yourself by treating agents and casting directors as objects of worship and desire. When you are a huge star, looking back on your beginnings, you will kick yourself for allowing them to crawl all over you and treat you as they do.

Start off on the right foot, with the psyche of the star, and don't let *anyone* push you around. And know that, bottom line, when it comes to agents in particular, you are always the one in charge.

D) IT'S BUSINESS!

It used to bother me to no end when agents would invite me to meet them, but then didn't ask, and declined my offer, to see a monologue. I would ask them dumbfounded, "But don't you want to see whether I can even act?" Now, I finally understand.

You see, agents don't care how great an actor you are. If they figure that you can book jobs for them and make them money, you've got yourself an agent. It's as simple as that.

You do *not* need to be a 'good' actor to get an agent, and that's the whole point that most actors fail to understand. Agents care whether you can make them money, and pay their bills. Hello! What have I been saying from the beginning? This is business, plain and simple!

You need to be marketable, and that's basically it. If it is apparent that you are being cast over and over again, or that you have some other unique quality... agents will want to work for you, casting directors will want to audition you, and producers will want to cast you.

If you put less effort into 'acting' and more effort into making your business marketable, guess what will quickly follow? That's right! SIGNAGE, BABY!

Don't worry if your agent hasn't a clue if you can act or what an acting genius you are. All you want from your agent are auditions, the ability to negotiate contracts, and the same ambition for your career that you have. That's *all* you need them to deliver. Heck, that is what they do! They get great auditions for actors and negotiate the contracts once you book the deals. If your agent can do that for you, then you snagged yourself a fab agent!

It's business. It's all about making money. It's all about whether you're marketable and bankable. That's all that matters. But can you act? That's for the press and the public to decide!

E) ON YOUR OWN

The longer I am in this business, the longer I begin to realize that most of the work I get is going to be entirely on my own, even though I am now working with some of the biggest agencies in Hollywood. Agents in my opinion are not there to create a career; they are there to negotiate contracts when you no longer have the time to do so.

Agents are nice and all, but they aren't the be all and end all. They are a means to an end, and if you get to the top of Hollywood without their help... so be it. If they do come into the equation—which probably will be the case—that is fine too!

What does this all mean? Agents are nice if you can get 'em, but no big deal if you can't! You do not *need* an agent to get your career going, or to keep it going. They may help, but they are not the linchpin to your success. Please understand that.

It's sort of like the song by U2: *With or Without You*. I'll succeed with agents... or I'll succeed without agents. One way or another I'll win that Oscar! I *can* live, oh great and wise agent, with or without you. And guess what: some people do! Some people just use lawyers to negotiate contracts for them—which is exactly what a large number of stars (and even up-and-coming stars) have done.

I guess my point is that while it might be harder and more difficult to do things on your own, it is important to realize that lack of an agent is most certainly not why someone does poorly in the arts. If you are doing poorly, and don't have an agent, it is *not* because you don't have an agent. If you are doing poorly, and *do* have an agent, it's *not* because you have a bad agent. If you are doing poorly, at any stage of your career—read this carefully now—it's because your number one agent (YOU!) has no idea what he's doing!

For example, how many of my readers have always wanted to write a book, but were overcome when thoughts of finding an agent came into the picture? How many of you decided not to even start writing for fear that no one would want to read it? How many of you actually followed through and *wrote* the book?

Everything comes full circle in this book, and the bottom line is always the same: IF YOU WANT TO DO SOMETHING, GET OUT THERE AND DO IT! DO IT NOW! STOP BEING LAZY! STOP COMING UP WITH EXCUSES! STOP BLAMING OTHERS FOR YOUR CIRCUMSTANCES! BLEK! YUCK! STOP IT! TAKE SOME RESPONSIBILITY FOR CRYING OUT LOUD!

You can't wait for someone else to make your dreams happen for you, and you can't wait for something—whatever that 'something' may be—to happen before you take that first step! Find some new and exciting way to make your dreams come true! NOW! Please? It's your future at stake here, ok?

F) NEGOTIATING YOUR OWN CONTRACTS

You need to know how to negotiate your own contracts. And yes, this applies even if you are signed with an agent, signed with a manager, and have an entertainment attorney on retainer. Why is this? It's because no matter what, *you* are always ultimately responsible as CEO and head attorney. Got it?

This means understanding basic contract law, being able to read and understand basic legalese (i.e. lawyer speak), and being able to tactfully point out and make counter-offers on points that you feel need revisions. No matter what project you may be involved with, you are setting yourself up for potential problems if you do not have a written and signed contract, both outlining what is expected of you, and also what you can expect from the other party. While some situations might warrant going forward without a contract, these situations are few and far between.

Once you do get cast (as you most certainly will), I absolutely insist that you draft your own contract, and act as your own agent, especially with regard to student films. I mention this because all too often there are directors out there who have no clue at all what they are doing (and this includes 'professionals' in many cases too)... and the last thing you want is to have to endure a hellish experience. I've endured too many of these... I don't want you to have to endure them too!

To avoid this happening, I started drafting contracts that the director had to agree upon before I accepted the part. If you are not careful, you will never receive a copy of the film on VHS or DVD; you will be forced to carry equipment and set up lights... and then perform; you will be asked to come back again and again for no pay, even when filming was scheduled to be over days ago...

Bottom line, you want to be a part of something worthwhile. If your director does not agree to these points below, he is obviously not very professional, and does not understand the importance of etiquette in business. If it scares off any potential director or producer... consider it a blessing: it probably would have been a nightmare of an experience to endure anyway. Use this list for reference, and consider them all when constructing your own contract. If writing up a full contract seems too much, at the very least, send the director and/or producer an email with the key points you insist upon, and make sure they respond with an 'OK' or some sort of documented approval. The key is to be crystal clear about expectations on both sides before pushing forward. It'll make the entire experience proceed that much more smoothly and efficiently. It'll also prepare you for your multi-million dollar negotiations in the future.

Essential Elements of an Independent Film Contract (which can be modified for use in theater, etc.)

1) Impart the ever-important rule that actors are not crew. No actor, union or otherwise, should be expected to help carry and set up equipment. That is not why they are using us. They are using us because we ACT, not because we CARRY. If you do

decide to help carry and set-up equipment, it is because you are doing them a *favor*. They need to understand this.

2) There should be no reason for actors to arrive early and have to wait three hours for the equipment to be set up. If the call time for actors is 6:00, then the crew should be there at 4, setting up, so when we arrive, they are ready to go.

3) Know what your shoot schedule is. Too often, a shoot schedule is poorly created, and because of this horrible disorganization, the film is only half-way shot when the pre-arranged shooting days are finished. Then the actor's whole schedule outside of filming is messed up because of having to keep coming back again and again. Say to them, "Now you said Thursday, Friday, and Sunday from 6 – 12, maybe a little later. Are you *certain* that this is enough time to shoot my scenes? Have you already made up storyboards, script breakdowns, and shot lists? Have you already secured film permits, scouted the locations, and figured out exactly how you are going to do this?" Know your plan... in advance. Know *their* plan... in advance. Know if you are going to have any rehearsals prior to shooting, and if the script is meaty, insist upon on it. For all the reasons above, I recommend all actors attend film school. Take Dov Simens' two-day film school (offered through UABS) or register at Digital Film Academy or NY Film Academy. It'll make you that much more of a savvy negotiator, not to mention that you'll also probably start shooting your own films and producing your own shows.

4) Make a point of insisting when on a non-paying film set that if the shoot does end up going over the pre-scheduled shooting days that you are compensated for any additional shoot days. This is done to ensure that there is no dilly-dallying on set. You want to arrive, get to work, and get it over with. After all is said and done, I am more than happy to be a part of a film for 'free', if it means a better reel, more connections, or increased exposure, but I can't be expected to simply keep coming back due to poor prior planning on the director's part. In other words... if shooting finishes on time, then no money is owed.

5) If you *are* getting paid in money... be sure to document how much and when payment is due. In case you're confused here, 'document' means IN WRITING & SIGNED!

6) Insist upon a GUARANTEED completion date, in writing, for the film. You do not want to put your time and effort into a film only to have it fall to the wayside. Be sure the director tells you why he is certain the film will be completed. What is *his* accountability?

7) Insist upon a GUARANTEED copy of the film on VHS or DVD (or whatever the latest technological advance may be), no later than one week from the final post production day of the film. If you do not, you will often end up with a credit... and no proof.

I hope I haven't scared you away with all of these demands, but all your time as an actor is business. I absolutely refuse to participate in any film or stage production anymore unless they are done with absolute professionalism, and this is how I run my own film shoots and stage productions.

Frankly, none of my 'demands' should come as a surprise; they are actually pretty obvious if basic film etiquette is followed. Perhaps you already know all of these things, but I can't assume that you do. And hey, perhaps the director/producer already knows these things... but you can't assume they do either.

As mentioned earlier, you must become your own agent. Dealing with directors and producers on your own, and on your own terms, is good practice overall for you as the businessman you are. It truly teaches you how to get what you want, and that's a lesson all professional actors should learn from day one.

Do *not* allow yourself to be pushed around by directors. These people are just like you but on the other side of the fence. Treat them with courtesy, but don't treat them as above you. They aren't. In fact, they are probably as nervous as you are because this may be the first time they are shooting a film or directing a play. Trust me—they probably aren't as far along as they would like you to believe they are.

Nonetheless—and this is a *big* nonetheless—directors and producers most certainly can help you, so don't be rude, and show some respect and appreciation. Besides, you never know where they might be heading in the future! If they go platinum… you'll certainly want to be on their side of the record when they do. So stick up for yourself, but don't sabotage your career with your outrageous demands. There most certainly is a line not to be crossed, and that line changes depending on a) how far along you are with your career, b) how far along the other side is with their career, and c) how persuasive a negotiator you are.

On that note, there is one key negotiating principle that I urge you never to forget. Ever. That rule is simple: *Everything Is Negotiable*. Even when someone tries to tell you that "It's non-negotiable," trust me—everything is negotiable. When someone tells you that something is non-negotiable, it simply means you haven't yet hit upon the point—or offered them that something—that *would* make it negotiable. Your mission as a pro negotiator is to determine whatever it is that would entice them to negotiate.

But again, it's a balance. Just because everything is negotiable doesn't mean you should always negotiate. Sometimes the best negotiation is the silent one where you don't push it.

P.S. # 1: Don't *ever* send off a signed contract without first making a photo copy of it. It may be a short-term hassle, but it'll end up being a long-term breath of relief. The one time you decide not to do this will inevitably be the one time you wish you had.

P.S. # 2: See *The Agent Matrix* in the annex for an in-depth analysis of client/representation relationships, and how this knowledge will help you get signed to the agent/manager/record label/publisher of your dreams.

CHAPTER FOURTEEN:

UNIONS

A) WHAT'S THE BIG DEAL?

Folks, getting into the unions really is not that big of a deal. I just want to make that clear to you up front. Just as agents are not an absolute prerequisite to success, neither are union memberships. I am proud to be a member of SAG, AFTRA, & EQUITY, but those memberships are not what have propelled my career forward. Not in the least.

While you should take advantage of every opportunity presented to join a union, do not worry too much about them. Just because you are in the unions does not mean that you are magically going to be working more. Unfortunately, it doesn't work like that. If it did, the statistics would be better. What statistics?

The stark reality that at any given time, the vast majority of union members (those in SAG, AFTRA, or EQUITY) *are not working*. Wild, eh? My point here is that getting into the unions shouldn't be a primary focus, nor should lack of membership be an 'excuse' for why you aren't more successful. The latter point is key, most notably because it is not that hard to get into the unions, which is the subject of the next section.

B) GETTING IN

Easy to get into the unions? Yes, very easy. Which is why it surprises me greatly when I meet people who have been in the business for more than two years who are *not* in the unions and try to tell me that they're *trying*. No, if you were really trying, you would be in the unions. Where there's a will there's way. Perhaps most importantly, if you are doing everything correctly, union membership will come simply as a matter of course. Just stop making excuses.

C) JOIN AFTRA

First step to getting into all the unions? Do as I did: JOIN AFTRA. Anyone can join. Spend the money now. Need some benefits of being in AFTRA? With this union membership you can:
- go to the AFTRA meetings and meet other union members, and become a part of one of the committees, if desired
- open an account with the Actor's Federal Credit Union
- be listed in the Academy Player's Guide in NY and the Academy Player's Directory in LA
- finally add a union to your resume
- secure your name in the AFTRA database so no other actor can take it
- take free acting classes and use AFTRA's facilities
- eat from the discounted Actor's Menu at the renowned Sardi's restaurant
- gain a whole lot of confidence by being a member of a professional actor's union
- blah blah blah blah blah… all good for you.

So join! And on a side note, you might want to look into GIAA (Italian American Actor's Guild) and HOLA (Hispanic American Actors Guild). Here's a hint: you don't need to be Italian or Hispanic to join either. Call them up and see what the benefits of joining might reap you. And while we're on the subject, there are probably a host of other unions you can join as well. Ask around! Be resourceful.

D) SAG/EQUITY

To get SAG and EQUITY, it's going to take a little more time, and a lot more effort and creativity, but it's not that difficult if you put your mind to it. I'm not going to get into the specifics here, because other books cover this topic very well, but I will say a few words.

If you start doing what this book prescribes with a totally gung-ho mentality, you might be surprised how quickly SAG & EQUITY union membership and other things come your way. While a six-month strive is certainly possible with most anything in this business, be prepared to update your projection every two months, and don't be surprised if it looks like it might take you longer than six months. The key is to know that you *are* making progress towards your goal.

In the first edition of this book, I wrote, "I wanted to be in EQUITY two years ago. I am still not, but instead I am in AFTRA and SAG. I'll be quick to say, though, that I have no excuse why I'm not in Equity. I should be working harder. The only reason I'm not in Equity is because it obviously isn't all that important to me. Nonetheless, I have no doubt that I will be in EQUITY very soon. Why? Because I'm doing so much that *not* to get into EQUITY would be impossible."

Today, I am in Equity and my feelings have not changed. If after two years, you are still not in all three unions, my recommendation is that you really should be working harder. The only reason someone is not in all three major unions is because they are actively choosing *not* to be (and I'm not sure why someone who proclaims to be an actor would choose *not* to be in all three unions) or because it obviously isn't all that important to him.

As long as you keep on chugging, do not give up, and aim for success, SAG and EQUITY *will* simply come as a matter of course.

If, though, after ten years of being in the business, you still aren't in all the unions, and still do not have an agent, then something is wrong.

It's far worse that your business failing. It's obvious that your business never even got off the ground.

If it's been ten years and you still are only in AFTRA, and still without a top notch agent... reread this book from the beginning, over and over, until every agent wants you and you are in every union that you want to join on the face of the planet.

I have no pity for 'pretend actors' who consistently fail to get anywhere because they are too lazy to make any real effort. If getting an agent and getting in the unions is really that important to you, figure out how to do it. Use your head, and stop making excuses. This isn't brain surgery. This is business.

Hint: See chapter 19.

E) BUT I DON'T WANT TO JOIN THE UNIONS!

Often times, I hear people say, "I don't want to join the unions because then I can't do non-union work." My response is always the same, "Why would you *want* to do non-union work?"

Let me tell you up front that if a production is non-union, it is *probably* (though not necessarily) very unprofessional. Yes, it is true that there are some non-union productions that *do* treat actors well, and that *do* have crews that know what they are doing... but they are few and far between. On the flip side, there *are* in fact also many union projects that are an embarrassment to be a part of. Yet, of all the projects I have worked on, in most cases, the unprofessionally run ones are typically... non-union. This is something to keep in the back of your mind. If you have to choose between a union and non-union job... the answer is union.

Now, that being said, I urge you to join every union as soon as you can. Why? Read on.

First, the unions are taking great strides to help make it easier for its members to participate in low budget opportunities. If you are in the unions, it's not that hard to find a union project that will meet your needs. There are so many different union contracts these days for nearly every type of budget imaginable that I find it rather amusing that there are in fact so many non-union films and shows. And this includes student films and plays.

Second, let's say you come across a really fantastic role... but the project is non-union. Problem, right? No! Not a problem! If you find a non-union project that you want to be a part of, simply make it part of your contract with the director and producer that the film must become union before you can work on it. If your marketing angle is solid and they are convinced that they need you, you're all set. Simple!

Better yet... do the paperwork FOR the director or producer to create your eligibility. It's really not all that difficult. To put together a SAG short film contract, it takes about 3 hours of paperwork. For a feature, it's a bit more involved, but certainly worth the effort if it means getting cast! It is very similar with Equity, AFTRA, etc. There are even contracts that actually allow union and non-union principals to work together on the same project. It's really not that big of a deal to make this happen. Just call up the union and tell them about the project and ask them what needs to be done in order for you to gain authorization.

Third, in most of the unions, you can 'opt-out' of membership for a period of time. I believe SAG calls it their 'CORE' program. If you absolutely must, you might be able to set up an arrangement such as this in order to work on a non-union production. At the very least, you should call up the union in question, explain your situation, and see how they may be able to accommodate you. Remember, unions *are* there to help you.

Fourth, and read this with a grain of salt so you don't get all huffy and puffy with me: how many people do *you* know who have been kicked out and banned from the unions? Now, let me make myself clear: I am not advocating that you join the unions and then expressly violate their 'rule number one', which is that you do not perform in non-union projects. In fact, up above, I just provided a number of ways for you to avoid doing just that.

However, what I am simply pointing out to you is the indisputable fact that there certainly are some union actors who *do* in fact do just this—because they are offered money; because they need tape for their reel; because it's a chance of a lifetime. I cite again the unfortunate statistic:

at any given time, most union actors are *not* working. I sometimes joke about this with people: the reason I think some union actors still do non-union work is because it helps them to pay their union dues!

Bottom line, as an entrepreneur, you need to know what you are up against and what your competition is doing. Knowing this, it is up to you to decide what the best course of action for your own career may be.

On that note, let me conclude by saying that I am grateful for what unions do for actors. The unions indeed are here to protect us, and so they do. They exist for us; not against us. The unions were created to ensure that actors aren't taken advantage of (as so often happens in non-union productions). And as I mentioned above, all of the unions are really taking great strides to help make it easier for producers to use union talent, and for union talent to participate in low-budget independent projects.

In conclusion, there really is no reason for you to ever do non-union work again after you become union. Why? Because it is not that hard to turn a non-union project into a union project, or to simply get 'authorization' from the union for you to participate in a non-union production. This is exactly why I urge you to join all of the acting unions as soon as possible, why people enjoy working more on union projects than non-union projects, and why I insist that you write up and negotiate contracts on any project that you are a part of… whether you are in a union or not.

CHAPTER FIFTEEN:

HEADSHOTS

A) DON'T WORRY, BABY!

Headshots are not as important as everyone says they are. Headshots are simply a way of people putting your name to a face. That's it.

Do you really think that stars care how great their headshots are? NO! If you've ever seen some star headshots, with the crazy lighting and funny eyes, you know what I am talking about. Everyone knows how the stars look, and the stars realize this. They understand that their headshot is not going to make or break their career. Nor will it make or break yours.

"Oh, but I'm not a star," you say. Well, start thinking like one, then! If you think the only thing standing in the way of your success is a silly little picture, then you are very misled. Most actors put such a heavy emphasis on their headshot because for them—that is the only tool they have at their disposal for 'getting a foot in the door'. What a shame. Me? I don't use just a static headshot to gain attention. No way. I use my charm, my killer marketing angle, my sizzling elevator pitch, and my amazing sales skills to get people to want to meet me. I can get meetings with agents and casting directors simply by calling them on the phone. What I actually look like is a 'bonus'.

For me, a headshot is not a door opener; but rather just a way to remind people who I am. And the sooner you remember this, the better off you will be, because you are *never—read NEVER—*going to be able to find a headshot that absolutely everyone likes. It is simply impossible because it is entirely subjective. I see far too many actors suffering and procrastinating because they think their headshot is bad. As a result, they don't send out their headshot, and they sit around and do nothing! Doing nothing is a very foolish thing to do.

If you are trying to 'get in the door' with the 'perfect' door-opening headshot, you may be setting yourself up for some truly heartwrenching disappointment. Here's my two-step process for headshot and acting success:

a) Get a headshot that you think is decent, and move on!

b) Start learning business, and become an amazing salesman. Start work on that amazing pitch that is going to get people salivating just to have the honor of meeting you.

B) FREE HEADSHOTS!

You'll notice that with some agents, no matter what headshot you have… they want you to change it. With others, you'll find they like the one you have. One agent likes this one, another that one, and on and on. The point is that everyone likes something else, i.e. it's subjective! Just as one person thinks I look like Richard Gere… another comes along who thinks I look like Pee Wee Herman. One person thinks I look like Eminem… another who thinks I look like Matthew Broderick. One person thinks I look like Robert DeNiro… another who thinks I look like John Cusac. One person thinks I look like Matthew Perry… another who thinks I look like David Schwimmer. You know what? I look a little bit like *all* of these people. I realize that it's all personal preference, and I deal with it. In fact, it might help you to know that when someone says you look 'like' someone, it actually usually means, 'you have a few qualities of' that person. That's why different people think you look like different people: they are seeing and pointing out different qualities.

On that note, it is *not* necessary to spend hundreds of dollars on headshots. Heck, you don't even have to pay for headshots. Have your friend take them, about 10 rolls. Do the processing at a local developer. You'll find a winner. Get them reproduced at a local developer. Kick some butt. Or get a digital camera and get your buddy to just keep on shooting until you find one that you like.

Find a friend, and go crazy! One of them will be great. If not, and none of them come out, then call up your pal and try again. It's *still* less expensive, and less of a headache, than going to a 'professional' photographer.

When my friends take my pictures, I am much more relaxed than I am when in a photographer's studio. Truly, how can you be relaxed with some strange dude you just met last week?

When you use a friend, there's no anxiety thinking, "Oh, what if they don't come out?!" With a friend… you can always shoot again… for free.

I guarantee no agent will know that your friend took it as long as you mirror what type of shot is currently in vogue. Just to prove a point, I bet that if you were to show shots your pal took of you to an agent and say that Mr. Big Photographer took them… he would likely believe you. In fact, for argument's sake, if you did that, and were indeed to mention a big photographer, simply because of the 'name-dropping', they'll probably look at the photo with a different eye and perceive it differently, for better or for worse.

Interesting, isn't it?

C) JUST A PICTURE!

If you really think that some stupid headshot is going to make or break your career, consider this:

Every once in a while, you see a star's headshot popping up in an advertisement for a certain photographer. Did this headshot make that person a star? I think not. If the headshot were so good and were destined to make that actor a star, the photographer would have used that headshot as publicity from day one. Am I right? Am I right?

I'm not telling you never to use a professional photographer. I'm just trying to make you understand that a headshot is *really* not all that important. It's a picture, for crying out loud! If after reading what I just wrote above, you still would prefer hiring a 'professional' photographer, by all means do so! Please, just don't spend an arm and a leg; don't add yourself to a six-month waiting list; and don't let them tell you how to do the shoot; etc. It's your money, and your time, and you really need to spend it wisely. If you're not rolling in the dough, I seriously urge you to find better places to spend your money than on overpriced headshots that are *not* going to make or break your career.

No matter how much you spend on headshots, some people will like them, and some won't. The same situation will arise if you end up using your friend's shots. Some people are going to love them, and some people are going to hate them. Deal with it.

So, in the final analysis, find someone to take your pictures (friend or foe-tographer), choose a decent shot, and start using it. Chances are it is just fine. Then, put that headshot out of your mind, and start worrying about more important things… like becoming a movie star!

CHAPTER SIXTEEN:
DON'T MOVE!

A) DON'T MOVE!

Ever heard the expression, "The grass is always greener..." Trust me... the grass may look greener elsewhere, but the truth is—and read this carefully—if you are not succeeding in one city, moving to another city is not going to magically make you more successful.

Truly, if you are struggling and having problems in NY, moving to LA is not going to help. And vice-versa.

Far too often, I meet fellow actors who are plodding along and failing miserably... who suddenly have a brainstorm: "A-ha! I am going to MOVE! Yes! Move! The problem is not with *me* and my lack of business sense; the problem is with *where I am living*! Of course that's it. Why didn't I think of this sooner! This is brilliant. Because there is far more work in NY <or> LA <or> Chicago <or> Toronto <or> Vancouver <or> London <or> Sydney, so... I am going to move there and watch my career soar!

That is the biggest crock of bull-oney I've ever heard. Please: whatever you do, unless you have a very clear and well thought out reason for moving... *do not move*. It's just going to set you back at least six months as you try to get re-acclimated to an entirely new city. Become successful where you are. If you cannot become successful where you are, you should re-evaluate—not the city in which you live—but the way you are approaching your entire career. If you're not making progress, don't embarrass yourself by blaming the city; take some responsibility and blame yourself, because it is *you* who is doing something wrong—not the city.

B) LA vs NY vs Chicago

La La land. The City of Angels. Loves Actors. Leave Amateurs. Lips & Ass. Los Angeles. Whatever you want to call it. All that matters is that you understand that just moving to Los Angeles means *nothing*. Big whooptie do. Congratulations: you are now the one billionth wannabe movie star who has just moved to Hollywood.

The Big Apple. The City That Never Sleeps. The Center of the Universe. New York City. Same deal: moving here means *nothing*. Congrats: now you are a tiny fish in a monstrous pond. Yee haw!

The Windy City. Chicagoland. My Kind Of Town. Second City. Chicago. Yup, same thing. Moving to Chicago really is nothing to be that proud of. You're just now one of many others who decided to do the same thing and the excitement is soon going to wear off.

Sure, rumor has it that those who really want to get into film should move to LA. That sort of makes sense since there are so many more movies being filmed there. But don't you also understand that there are also that many more actors competing for the same roles? So, wouldn't it make more sense to get into the films in NY? Ahh, but alas, there aren't as many films being shot in NY.

What about Broadway? If you want to hit the boards, everyone knows to come to NY. But again, this is where everyone comes to get onto Broadway.

So what about getting involved in Chicago, or in the 99-seat theaters in LA? Less competition, surely. But less shows too.

You see the point I am trying to make: the grass is always greener. There is no 'perfect' place to make your career. You hear one story of a film-maker moving out to LA to make his dream come true… and then you hear about Kevin Smith who not only shot his first film in Jersey, but still lives there today. You hear one story about someone moving to NY and becoming a huge Broadway star... and then find Julia Roberts crashing onto center stage from Hollywood.

Folks, there is far more than one way to skin this show business cat. TRUST ME: where you are currently living really has no bearing on your success or your failure. Even if you are currently living in the middle-of-nowhere, USA, you are still capable of launching a Hollywood or Broadway career without moving. How so? Here are some scenarios:

a) You write a screenplay, start a production company, film it with you as the star, submit it to festivals, and win first prize. Voila.

b) You write a screenplay, get repped by a Hollywood agency, and sell it—thus launching your career by getting your foot in the door.

c) You start an equity theater wherever you are, and put on a play that gets so much regional attention that the show ends up going national.

The possibilities are absolutely endless.

Where you are currently living has *nothing* to do with your current success or failure. It is not the place, but the person. *YOU* my friend are the one who is responsible.

No matter where you are, if you are thinking about moving, please ask yourself this one question first, "Have I truly done everything possible (and I mean *everything*) to make a success out of myself in this current city in which I am living?"

Let me clue you into the answer: THE ANSWER IS NO, every single time. Think about that.

And don't you *dare* move to another city because some agent is 'interested' or some casting director said you have 'potential'. It's a recipe for disaster. If it's a sure thing, move. In most cases, it is not.

There are only a few scenarios that I consider valid reasons for moving:

a) A legitimate agent or manager actually *signs* you to a representation contract.

b) You are cast in a major show and/or film. Major = paid, national exposure, and a great role.

c) You are so wealthy, business savvy, and creative that when you arrive in the new city, you can monopolize the media with amazing ROI advertising that makes you the glowing talk of the town upon your arrival. If you don't know what ROI advertising is, then this option definitely does not apply to you. ☺

d) You have an indisputable valid business reason for needing—not wanting—to go. "Better opportunity" is usually not a valid reason. Nor is, "More projects" or "More roles".

Bottom line, I am just trying to look out for you. Of course, sometimes moving may be the best option for you to take... but nine times out of ten, I find people are not—as they claim—moving towards opportunity. Rather, they are actually running as fast as they can from adversity, and from the brutal reality that success in business is *really really hard*. In fact, success in *show* business is even harder, where the demand for talent is depressingly low and the supply is absolutely inexhaustible.

Don't run from the challenge. Stand up to whatever city you are in and show her who is boss! If you are going to succeed in show business, you need to learn how to control the city; don't you dare let the city you are in control you.

C) GOING INTERNATIONAL

This is a very short section because I really only have a few things to say on the subject of going international: Go for it!

First off, we all know you are going to become a movie star and stage star... and that implicitly also means that you are also going to have an international fanbase. So... why not start cultivating it now and preparing for the future?

Are you marketing internationally? Do you have an Italian fan club? If not, why not start it now? Are you getting involved with the online film and stage communities in other countries? Are you investigating exactly what it is going to take to get your film into the Cannes Film

Festival, or to be invited onto a French talk show to talk about the newest films? Think big! Despite what you may believe, you are *very* close to international stardom right at this very moment. You need to realize this. Otherwise you might be shocked when it happens, and I'd hate to see you crumble under the stress and pressure.

Second, there are a *lot* of acting opportunities in Canada, England, & Australia (not to mention a ton of equally exciting theatrical projects going on in every other country in the world as well). Now, you might think I am contradicting myself by recommending you consider these other opportunities based on what I wrote in the previous chapter, but on the contrary, I am not. I am not telling you to move there. I am in fact just trying to point out that you shouldn't neglect castings going on in Canada, England, Australia, and elsewhere. Moreover, if you speak a foreign language, you might want to investigate how the film/stage industry works in countries that speak that language. I have a handful of friends who live in America but do voiceovers for foreign markets, and are even flown overseas for shoots for weeks at a time. In fact, if you can play the 'stupid American tourist' in some foreign film, you might not even have to know the foreign language that the film is shot in!

My point: there are *so many damn opportunities out there*! All *you* have to do is exploit them.

D) GETTING A GREEN CARD FOR THE US

Hey all you foreigners trying to make it in Hollywood and on Broadway: *if you can't figure out how to get a visa and how to stay in the country, how the heck do you expect to be able to break through and stay in Hollywood and on Broadway, huh?*

If I hear one more person tell me that the reason they didn't *make it* in show business is because their Visa expired or because they couldn't get a visa in the first place, I am going to blow a gasket. This excuse is just as bad as the 'if only I had an agent I'd be getting cast' or the 'if I were in the unions, things would be different' racket.

There are so many different stories I have heard of people who have managed to figure out how to get a visa and stay in the United States that it made this section necessary. In fact, it doesn't even matter if you can't get a visa. Why is that? If you don't know the answer, you might want to re-read the previous chapter on 'NOT MOVING!'

Quick Reminder: I tried to crash the Cannes Film Festival in 1998, and for six hours, I was denied. I could have given up as many did before me. Instead I vowed to 'find my visa' and through my determination and creativity, I managed to act my way in and become an 'associate producer' on a film. Where there's a will, there's a way, folks. Don't let 'lack of a visa' be the excuse that haunts your past, hinders your present, and mars your future. Your dreams are too important to allow excuses get in the way. Your grandchildren don't want to hear the 'Did you know that I used to be an actor, Tommy' story. No, they want to hear the, "Grandma/Grandpa, tell me again how you took Hollywood and Broadway by storm and got invited to the White House" story.

I see you nodding your head in agreement, so I am glad you see my point. ☺

CHAPTER SEVENTEEN:

SOME OTHER
THINGS TO CONSIDER

A) GETTING ON LETTERMAN, CONAN, & LENO

Hey, stop kidding yourself, ok! Please, stop being so 'safe' by arguing that you don't want to become a star. That's a lie. If you are in show business as a performer, it's because you *love* the attention. Don't run from that and don't deny that love.

Yes, I know it is easier to say that you don't want stardom—that you just want to be a 'working' actor—but that's a joke. No one just wants to be a working actor, and if the only thing you are striving for is 'working actor', then you are going to end up being a 'starving actor' by default, because no one *ever* gets what they want; they almost always get one notch less.

In other words, if you really do just want to be a 'working actor' (and I hope you don't want just that), then you need to shoot for *more* than that: you need to shoot for stardom, and part of that means working towards appearing on the national talk shows.

Now, getting onto the late night talk shows is in many ways a true measure of your progress. Once you are invited to appear as a guest or to perform on Letterman, Conan, Leno, Ellen, Oprah, Carson Daly, Craig

Kilborn, or a multitude of other talk-shows, it means—undeniably—that you are on your way. It shows that you are getting closer and closer to becoming a star.

Getting onto the talk shows, though, is only half the battle. Getting invited back again is key as well. And therein lies the challenge.

While most people might think an appearance on late-night means you have 'arrived', those in the know, know better. You see, last I checked, there is actually a rating system for guests, not dissimilar to the Nielson ratings for television shows. In other words, yes, if you appear as a guest on a television show, there are companies that actually rate your 'public appeal' in an effort to determine whether you are invited back again.

In other words: you may have 'arrived', but only at the port of embarkation. You may be on the verge of stardom... but only the verge. If an acting analogy is easier to understand, your appearance on a national talk show is really just another... audition. An audition before America.

Whether the rating system is exactly as I describe is irrelevant. What is relevant is that getting on one of these talk shows is not only something to strive for, but something that can help launch or ground your career. So do whatever you can to get onto one of these talk shows... and then take the opportunity very seriously once you do.

So how do you get on these talk shows? The key—as always—is to be different.

Consider what makes a great guest. Take a few nights to watch these talk shows, and I think you'll know immediately which guests are going to be invited back again, and which are not.

In nearly all cases, those guests invited back are *cool*. When I say cool, it's more than just an aura. It's the entire way about them. And in my opinion, a large part of being cool is having a great story to tell and being a great story teller. And those with the greatest stories... are those who broke the rules.

In other words, if your aim is to get onto one of these shows... and be invited back, one clear strategy would be to do something ambitious, amazing, in a different way, breaking all the rules in the process... and succeed. Now that would be an amazing story. And it would naturally follow that the person behind this story would be quite an amazing guest.

So… think! What can you do with your career that's different enough to get the attention of these talk shows? What can you do that is ambitious, amazing, different, and that breaks all the rules? The answer might be just enough to set you apart from your competition, and help you move ahead to the next level.

B) PAY TO MEET INDUSTRY? YOU ARE INDUSTRY.

Stop paying to audition. That is just disgusting. Don't you have any respect for yourself? Don't you believe that you have more to offer than just your money? Do you think you can buy your way into the hearts and minds of the American movie and theater going public? You can't.

You should not have to pay to audition. Bottom line. That is just deplorable.

Truly, where do these companies get off charging *you* to meet agents & casting directors. In fact, I find it more than a bit distasteful that agents and casting directors accept money from talent in return for meetings under the guise of 'education'. It's baloney. A rip-off. Sleezy. Disgusting. Wrong!

It is absurd when I see ads for a 'Meet Industry' night and discover (what a big surprise!) that everyone *but* the actors get in for free. Doesn't that seem to give you a subtle signal that unlike everyone else, you are not industry yourself?

That's preposterous! You ARE industry! Without you—the actor—there *is* no industry! Without you—the actor—Hollywood and Broadway cease to exist! If we're talking about power here, you the actor have quite a bit of it and I frankly am sick and tired of agents and casting directors and producers and directors and other 'holier than thou' SIPID losers trying to make actors feel like worthless pieces of BLEEP! How about you? Are you with me on this?

Don't pay to meet industry. Even if it means taking an extra year or two (or five) to get to the top, don't sell your soul just to become successful. To me, paying to audition is almost like hiring a prostitute:

you can't get any 'interviews' on your own through your own business prowess, so you decide to pay for an interview, because in the short-term, it makes you feel better about yourself and less like a failure. Then, you find out a year later that you have the artistic and business equivalent of STDs, and it hits you like a ton of bricks that your whore didn't love you or care for you at all: SHE JUST DID IT FOR THE MONEY.

C) HOW TO WIN AN OSCAR AND TONY.

First off, I think it's a noble ambition to strive for an Oscar and Tony, and I know that quite a few of you reading this book are going to win not one, but two or more! I support you one hundred percent. Heck, even I am striving for an Oscar & a Tony.

Here is the secret prerequisite to winning an Oscar:

YOU FIRST NEED TO PLAY AN OSCAR-CALIBER ROLE IN AN OSCAR-NOMINATED FILM!

Here is the secret prerequisite to winning a Tony:

YOU FIRST NEED TO PLAY A TONY-CALIBER ROLE IN A TONY-NOMINATED FILM!

You might think I am oversimplifying this, but ladies and gentlemen, you simply cannot win an Oscar or Tony as an actor in any other way!

You see, the problem with most actors is that they *say* they want to win an Oscar or Tony, but if you ask them what they are specifically doing to *win* an Oscar or Tony, they are speechless, or worse, say, "Well, I'm hustling; auditioning; getting my name out there."

No, No, NO! What are you specifically doing to win an Oscar or Tony? Are you writing an Oscar-winning screenplay or show in which you can play a lead or supporting role? Did you hire someone else to write an Oscar or Tony-winning role for you? Did you write a 'bubble gum' film that you *know* is going to become a success in Hollywood and America—just so that someone then hires you for an Oscar or Tony caliber role? Are you researching every single upcoming film and show and analyzing them for Oscar/Tony-winning potential, and doing all that you can to get into these projects? Have you done your research to determine what it took for the 'typical' Oscar or Tony winning actor to get cast in that role? Did they create the role themselves? Did someone else cast them? Who cast them? Why? Why were they nominated? Why did they win? Read that last question again: Why did they win?

In many cases, the answer is not, "because they gave the best performance." No, often the answer is, "politics." Politics: because they should have won last year; because the 'best' actor was recently involved in a scandal; because friends vote for friends; etc.

If you really want to win an Oscar or Tony... *get off your ass and start working harder than every single other actor in the world.* OK?

Now, it's important to understand that few people actually remember what actors win Oscars and Tonys for anyway. Winning an Oscar or Tony for an amazing performance is often only remembered for the 'winning' part, rather than the 'amazing performance.' So, you have to ask yourself, "why do I *really* want to win an Oscar or Tony?"

There are a few good reasons for wanting to win (or even just be nominated for an Oscar or Tony): First, you'll get paid a lot more. Second, your credibility will skyrocket. Third, you'll get more publicity. Sure, it really doesn't necessarily mean you *were* the best actor, but more money, credibility, and publicity can sure do a lot of good in terms of opening doors and creating opportunities!

Or does it?

On one hand, it gives you more money, credibility, and publicity, but those things also come with a price. You see, winning also sets you up for potential failure because now you're an "Oscar Winner", and with that comes a certain expectation for excellence. There are countless stories of the so-called Oscar & Tony curse—once you win, your career tanks. This happens in many cases because producers start to feel you are 'too important' and 'too expensive' for their production, and subsequently don't consider you for fear of being turned down. Or, when you are cast, everyone expects such an amazing performance from you that any deviation from that standard is considered a crowd-pleasing letdown.

My point is that while I do believe you absolutely should be striving for an Oscar and Tony—remember Times Two & Tomorrow?—you need to also realize that you can have an amazing superstar career even if you never even get nominated. There are many actors who indeed have such careers who have never even won an Oscar. Keanu Reeves—one of my all-time favorite actors—is the first that comes to mind.

Bottom line, an Oscar or Tony, like anything else, has its pros and cons. Be very careful what you wish for; you just might get it.

CHAPTER EIGHTEEN:
BY THE WAY

A) YOUR WEBSITE

You need a website. It's as simple as that. Don't gawk. You are not an actor, but a businessman, remember? If you don't know anything about computers... you had better learn! What kind of business these days doesn't use a computer?

My dad is an 80-year old WWII veteran who grew up in the depression when the TV was just being invented, and even *he* uses a computer for his business nowadays. *Everything* is going digital, and if you don't have a website, your competition is quickly going to leave you in the dust.

Why do you need a website? Simple. A visitor to your website will be able to a) read your biography and latest news, b) browse your photo gallery, c) see your resume, d) listen to your voice-over demo, e) watch your reel, f) listen to monologues, g) and then contact you. A well set-up website could feasibly book you a job. Mine has done just that. Check it out at www.monroemann.com or alternately www.FutureOscarWinner. com. ☺

Keep in mind that you don't want just any old website. It doesn't have to be super fancy, but it does have to be well thought out, carefully planned, beautifully designed, fully functional, and constantly up-to-date with current information and news. You want a reliable server with service that you can count on and the peace of mind knowing that there are no third-party ads interfering with the message you are trying to impart.

You see, you want total control of site content, you want an easily memorable web address, and the peace of mind that only money can buy. Your site cannot be housed on a free server. Nothing looks more lame. You do not want third-party ads on your site. In other words, you don't want a subsidiary, i.e. free, URL. To get rid of the ads, you need to pay. Suck it up.

That's right! You have to fork over even more money for this acting career of yours. Who would have thought! It will cost no more than about $30 to register your domain name for two years, and then about $25 per month to host the website. I use GoDaddy.com, and they are reputably one of the best. Verio.com is another good one. To date I have not had any problems with either.

Some of my sites I construct myself, and I do all of the updates myself. It's really very simple. Read a few books, learn how to use a computer, and learn how to design websites yourself. Alternately, you can hire someone else to do it for you, which I have done with some of my more advanced sites, given my increasing lack of time. Just remember this: Outsourcing control of your website may be a great time saver, but in some cases, it can be more of a pain in the butt than a time-saver. Weigh your decision carefully.

You can also go ahead and use third party 'acting' websites to house your headshot, resume, and reel, and perhaps benefit from their reputation. However, you are losing out on many potential customers because many won't have the patience to find your page. It takes a long time to find these 'subsidiary' pages, and it likely isn't easy to remember your web address either. How much easier is it to remember monroemann.com, than Actorpages/home/actors/males/monroe.html?

B) EXTRA WORK

What about extra work? Don't worry: you will not be typed solely as an extra. That is totally absurd. If you are up for a great speaking role, and are right for the part, no one will care whether you did extra work last week.

One of my students, Doug Williams, has used extra work as a great stepping stone. This powerhouse of a guy produced his own show, broke a Guinness world-record as a publicity stunt for it, and then ended up singing live on *Carson Daly* that very night because of it. Singing live on *Carson Daly*. Wow! And even *he* still does extra work. Why? Because he meets people like George Clooney and Matt Damon.

You see, he did extra work because he knew where it could lead, and lead to places it did! He ended up becoming Clooney's stand-in for an entire film, and Damon's for another. Did they chat? But of course! And he can call both of them friends now. Because—ta da—of extra work.

I even have my own extrawork story to share with you. If you saw the movie *Swimfan*, then you might remember Erika Christensen's ex-boyfriend, Jake Donnelly. You know, the guy in the coma that comes back to life in the end?

Well... that's me. That part gave me my very first credit in a 'real' movie, and got me listed on the Internet Movie Database as a result. That part also resulted in giving me the inspiration to start my own production company and write my screenplay, which likely would never have come to pass otherwise. That part also helped me to truly feel like a part of 'Hollywood'. And, yes ladies and gentlemen, that part started out as... an extra role given to me by Kee Casting in NY.

I responded to an ad in—guess what?—*Backstage*. What started out as just another extra job turned into the turning point of my career. They were looking for guys with swimmer bodies. Well, my photo got in front of the producers and they determined that I looked like the leading man of the movie, Jesse Bradford. Soon, I was meeting the producer, then the director, then Erika Christensen. Next thing I know, I'm walking the streets of NY with Erika, hand in hand, as her 'boyfriend', eating ice scream, laughing, talking—all while the still cameras took photos of us for the film. Over the next three weeks, I am shooting the film, going to parties at the producer's house, playing cards with Jesse Bradford, Shiri Appleby, Jason Ritter, and the list goes on.

My point is that what started out as extra work gave me my first legitimate film role in a movie. And when I'm on Leno, Conan, and Letterman, just as Kevin Costner's first role was the dead body in *The Big Chill*, so mine is the comatose guy in... *Swimfan!* (except I get to come to life in the end, so already I have one up on Costner). Ha ha. "And yes Monroe," says the host, "we do have a clip..."

So go ahead and do extra work if you've got nothing else to do, even if your agent says otherwise. Extra work affords you the opportunity to be on a film set, to get paid, and to eat free food. More importantly, you might just get bumped up to a larger role, and you might just meet someone who can do something for you (both of which happened to me and countless others).

In the first edition, I wrote the following, "Extra work is great! When people ask me why I do extra work even though I am often called for principal roles, I say, 'There is always something to be gained. I hope to meet other people, other winners, like me.' I always do. Enough said." Today, do I still read *Backstage* as voraciously as I once did, and do I still do extra work? No, I admit that. But this is the key you need to understand: it is *not* because I believe I am too far along to do it, or too important to do it. It is because *I am too busy* to do it! Busy playing with my band, producing my films, writing my books, speaking on the college circuit, and making my dreams come true.

Now, do I still have a subscription to *Backstage?* The answer to that is yes. And do I still read it each week. Yes, I do. Because ya never know what film or play might be in there. And would I still do extra work if I were called? Absolutely, if I am available. If I have a free day to make an extra $150 - $300 and also pass out some information about my school and spread the word about my film, of course I'll do it. I'd be an idiot not to. You need to understand that.

While a lot of extra work itself is boring and unlikely to catapult you into stardom, the connections you make along the way may very well do just that. When on a set, I always make a point to try to introduce myself to *everyone*, even the head director.

Don't be scared. Get some guts, walk up to Mr. Big Director, extend your hand, and say, "Hi! I'm Joe Actor, pleased to meet you!" Say your name loudly, clearly, and confidently! And try to throw in your marketing angle and claim to fame as well. Tactfully, mind you.

Do that with *everyone*, then call the production office, get the crew list, and start sending thank you notes, starting with the words, "It was a pleasure to meet you today on the set of …" Wow! Look at that! You just made connections!

Don't become a self-important prima donna and refuse extra work flat-out. You may be throwing away valuable connections. Nor become the type of person who '*only* accepts principal work', even though not currently working. Talk about really being cocky… and stupid. So, what, you're just going to sit around and wait for that principal work to come to you? The only time you should refuse extra work is when you are so busy with principal work that it is *impossible* to do both.

There are truly great opportunities lurking in the background, and the Unstoppable Artist will exploit a day on a set for all it is worth. (You may, though, want to steer clear of non-union extra work. That's no fun. And yes, even if you are not SAG, you can still be an extra in a SAG movie. Call SAG and find out more.)

C) TYPE

What type are you? Screw them all! You, my fellow actor, are whatever type you think you are!

Obviously if you weigh 20 lbs, you won't play the 2000 lb lead, but on the whole, looks are very subjective. Someone's beauty to one person is to another person ugliness. More importantly, type is more often a measure of subjective single traits than a true measure of a person as a whole. In other words—as I mentioned briefly earlier in the book—if someone says you look 'like' someone or 'remind' him of someone, it usually doesn't mean you are a dead ringer; it simply means you have a few similar characteristics of that person.

In other words, if they are looking for a male, and you are a male, you are right for it. If they are looking for a blond, and you have brown hair, who cares, because you are right for it. If they are looking for a gorgeous model type girl, I don't care what you look like, because gosh darn it, you are right for it. If they are looking for a guy, and you are a girl, should you go for it! Absolutely! It seems every day there are new gender bender projects popping up. Whether it's the best direction for art as a whole, this *is* showbusiness where there are no rules, so why not: you are right for it!

While in the beginning, some people will feel you are best typed into this or that category... for the time-being, just go with it. You can always branch out later. Check out Tom Hanks. He sure plays the romantic and hero roles rather well, but initially, everyone thought he would never play leading roles like that. He sure proved them wrong. Go Unstoppable Actor!

Regardless of what anyone tells you, do not feel that you will never be a leading man, or that you will never be anything but the best friend. You can be whatever you want to be! Someone out there will believe in your dreams too. And if not... make your own stinkin' movie.

Save up some money, write a screenplay, cast yourself as the debonair lead, film it, produce it, sell it, market it, win an Oscar, then revel in the glory! Yeah baby, Yeah! Hooah!

Type what? Type THIS!

CHAPTER NINETEEN

THE QUICKEST WAY TO THE TOP

A) PRODUCE!

I decided to save my best advice for the end. As many of you know, I started out as a 'regular actor', with headshots, resumes, auditions, agents, and casting directors. I went through the struggle for years—it's important to pay your dues a bit, I suppose. But then I had enough.

And when you've had enough, I urge you to start producing. And sooner than later is probably some pretty sound advice.

Every major star produces their own projects. Adam Sandler has Happy Madison productions. Oprah has HARPO (which is Oprah backwards, in case you didn't know). Drew Barrymore has her own production company called Flower Films; Will Smith has his own production company too. So does Clint Eastwood. This list is endless. If you intend on making a huge success of yourself, the key word is PRODUCE!

For years, I refused to do any such thing because I wanted someone *else* to discover my amazing talent. It soon became quickly obvious to me that if I wanted to become a movie/stage star… I would have to learn how to become a producer. And so I did. And my life and career have never been better.

For years, I would try to get the little boutique agencies in NY to consider working with me... to no avail. Now, as a producer, I am talking, negotiating, and working with Creative Artists, Endeavor, William Morris, United Talent Agency, and the list goes on. Why the sudden interest in me? Well, *no one* wants to talk to an actor; but everyone will take the time to speak with a producer who also happens to be an actor. And the result has been that those very boutique agencies I wanted to work with before... are now calling *me* asking to set up appointments for me *as an actor* (not a producer). Cool, eh?

In fact, remember this important lesson: *never say the word.* Never tell someone that you are an actor. It's just like in negotiation: whoever says the first number first loses. Same thing here, except whoever says the word actor last wins. In other words, you want *the other person* to bestow the title of actor upon you. When *they* call you an actor... it is a title of respect. When *you* call yourself an actor... it is a title of derision, shame, and embarrassment. This is so because most 'actors' are losers. Waiters. Temps. Bums. Everything *but* professional actors.

When someone *does* ask you what you do for a living, the answer is not 'I'm an actor', but rather, 'Well, right now, I am playing the role of a doctor in a film being shot in New York." You see the difference? You alleviated their fear by proving that you are *not* just another loser actor, but rather, are a true winner who is currently actually acting! What a novel concept. And can you guess what this person's next question to you is going to be? Yup, you got it, "So... you're an actor?" BOOM, they said the word. When *they* say it... it must be true. Shazam.

Remember: Actors starve; Movie & Broadway stars make money. Don't *ever* be an actor. Be a producer/actor! It's a heck of a lot cooler (and infinitely more profitable).

B) SO HOW DO I PRODUCE?

There are a number of ways that you can easily get involved with producing.

Here is a short list:

- WRITE YOUR SCREENPLAY
- PRODUCE YOUR FILM OR PLAY
- WRITE YOUR ONE-MAN SHOW
- START YOUR BAND/MUSICAL ACT
- WRITE YOUR DAMN BOOK ALREADY!

That last one isn't really a performance art at all, but I would be remiss if I didn't tell you that writing and publishing a book, and getting it widely distributed is one of the best credibility building tools you can create for yourself. You also saw up there the proposal to write your own screenplay and get it produced with you playing a role. Or producing a film or play written by someone else in which you cast yourself. Or putting together a one-man show than you mount yourself in one of the tens of reputable theaters in NY, LA, and elsewhere. Maybe starting a band or a musical act is your best bet? With you in the lead singing role?

This list is truly endless. There are so many ways to produce a career for yourself that it is truly inexcusable of you to just 'pursue auditions' and then give up, exasperated, convinced that you gave it your all. True, you may not *want* to produce, but come on! Success is not a right; it is a privilege. You are entitled to *nothing*. NOTHING.

If you really want to succeed as an actor, then do whatever you need to do to make that happen, ok? Success is all about sacrifice people! How truly obsessed are you? Does success mean enough to you that you are willing to do whatever is necessary to make your dreams come true? I certainly hope so. 'Cause your future sorta depends on it.

TO THE THEATRICAL JUGGERNAUT

If after all is said and done, you don't agree with anything I say in this book, Cheers! There are no rules! If you have a better way of doing it, go for it!

If you think you can get by without a headshot, I'm with you! If you only want to do film, and you hate theater more than anything in this world, then succeed on your terms, and throw theater to the side! If you refuse to ever use a computer or a cell phone, and hate the Internet and websites, then figure out some other way to do it! Heck, I don't even care if, as they say, you are in this business 'for the wrong reasons'!

If you simply want fame and fortune... go for it! If you merely want to impress your friends, cheers! Heck, if you are just drawn to the challenge of doing something that everyone says can't be done, go for it!

There are no wrong reasons, and there are no rules. If you want to do it... go out there and do it, on your terms, and according to your rules.

I will say this, however. It's about your _why_.

If you don't have a strong enough WHY that is driving you to success, then your arrival there is going to be very empty indeed. While fame and fortune may be something you are striving for, that shouldn't be the end in itself. You need to have a far more giving reason for wanting success; something that has nothing to do with you and everything with helping others.

Truly, the most successful people in the world get there… by helping others. You might, then, be wondering what *my* 'why' is. It is simple: I want—and am going—to become a rich and famous movie star and rock star **because** (this is my why), only then will I be able to help inspire *millions* of people to realize that nothing is impossible and that their dreams really can come true. My success in the arts is only going to add more and more credibility to Unstoppable Artists Business School, and the more credible the school is, the more students I am going to be able to entice through its doors. For me, my God-given calling is inspiring people to overcome obstacles. I can do this best through fame and fortune as a movie star and rock star. Make sense? It's not all about me. And *that* is a 'why' that has the power to propel to the greatest heights. So what is *your* why?

And while you're pondering that, it's important for you to know that it's just a matter of time before anyone who is really trying succeeds. Just keep chugging, and don't let anyone or anything get you down… and you *will* get there. Persistance: It's the centuries-old recipe for success. Just don't confuse persistence with insanity: which is doing the same thing over and over again expecting different results. ☺

Bottom line: *YOU* are at the helm of your future. *YOU* are the one who is determining your fate. *YOU* are the master of any misfortune that you perceive blocks your path.

Remember, as Yoda once said, "Try not. Do, or do not. There is no try." There is no excuse for your failing.

You are on the verge of kicking some major theatrical butt! You are now, if you choose to accept the privileged title,

A THEATRICAL JUGGERNAUT.

Now, go out there and kick it!
And… meet you at the top!
-Monroe Mann
Founder, Unstoppable Artists Business School
roe@unstoppableartists.com
www.FutureOscarWinner.com
www.UnstoppableArtists.com
1-888-YSTARDOM

A FEW PARTING WORDS:

a) If you liked this book and it helped your career, please be sure to post a glowing review up on Amazon.com and BN.com. It would really mean a lot to me!

b) Tell your friends to buy a copy for themselves, or better yet, give a copy to your friends. You *know* they need to read it.

c) Contact Unstoppable Artists Business School today to find out about how you can attend our next FREE class audit either in person or by phone, and about our 'guaranteed results' mentoring program. You can also receive our FREE seven-day email business course by signing up to our mailing list at www. UnstoppableArtists.com

d) Please email me! Tell me how you like the book! My email address is right up above and I love to hear from those people who I might be working with one day. I'll be sure to get back to you as soon as I possibly can. ☺

e) Actually, the book isn't really over yet. *Keep on reading!*

PART C:

THE ANNEX

REQUIRED READING LIST

(with book reviews)

NOTE: You can conveniently purchase most of these books (and more) at our very own online business bookstore: www.UABSBooks.com. We have partnered up with Amazon.com to make your shopping experience as easy as possible. If you are looking for the finest selection of attitude and business books to help you get to the top as quickly as possible… look no further than our Unstoppable Artists Business School Book Store, at UABSBooks.com.

A) THE FIRST BUNCH OF BUSINESS BOOKS YOU SHOULD READ

(You can find these business books and hundreds more for convenient sale at UABSBooks.com under the 'start here' tab)

- *Rich Dad Poor Dad* & *Cashflow Quadrant*
  Both by Robert Kiyosaki & Sharon Lechter

Those who read these books and do not understand them, or disagree with them, have serious mental problems. They should check themselves into a mental hospital immediately. These are two of the finest personal finance books I have ever read. Ignore reading them at your own peril.

- *Battle Cries for the Underdog*
  By Monroe Mann

This guy is a complete and utter wacko, and I would steer clear of anything written by him. ☺ Oh wait, that's me! Be sure to read this book. It's the one I wrote while in Iraq. It is also the first self-help book to come out of modern combat, and I know you'll enjoy it. G. Gordon Liddy says it is 'filled with some of the finest insights to be found in history' and Jay Conrad Levinson calls it 'profound'.

- *Guerrilla Marketing*
  By Jay Conrad Levinson

This book got me hooked on marketing. Sort of like 'hooked on phonics', but more business focused. ☺ This man is the founder of guerrilla marketing and his series is officially the best-selling marketing series of all times, with over 14 million copies sold. There is a reason for that. Don't miss this book! P.S. – I am co-writing two books with Jay, one entitled, "Guerrilla Networking" and the other entitled, "Guerrilla Marketing for the Arts". And if rumors hold true, I am mentioned in the acknowledgements of the 4th edition of *Guerrilla Marketing* as one of the 'World's Greatest Guerrillas'. And this book, *The Theatrical Juggernaut*, also happens to be listed in his bibliography. Groovy, eh?

- *Guerrilla PR*
  By Michael Levine

The famous Tiffany principle: Perception is more important than reality. Never forget that, and be sure to pick up this book. It's an excellent primer on publicity written by one Hollywood's most prolific publicists. He's a great guy to know. FYI, sign up for his Levine Breaking News (LBN) Email Updates. If you're in the know… you are on this list.

- *Multiple Streams of Income*
  By Robert Allen

Most artists struggle day after day trying to survive off of a meager income until their 'big break'. Don't live like that! Begin creating your multiple streams of income today! This book can help. That's an understatement.

- *What Rich People Know & Are Desperately Trying to Keep Secret*
  By Brian Sher

Wouldn't you like to know what the secret is? Of the over 500 business books in my personal library, none is more highlighted than this one. Brian is a wonderful person whose book should be at the top of your list to read!

- *24 Essential Lessons for Investment Success*
  by William O'Neill

We were talking about multiple streams of income up above. One of those streams absolutely should be the stock market. This book was the first to truly help demystify what the stock market was all about and I've been making money ever since!

- *Building Wealth One House At A Time*
  By John Schaub

Sometimes, the title just says it all. Real Estate is one of the most lucrative forms of wealth building. If you are not yet involved in real estate investment... now is the time. Start by reading this book.

- *Selling the Invisible*
  By Harry Beckwith

So many people in the arts think they are selling a product. Yuck! No! In most cases, you are selling a SERVICE. And when you are selling a service… you are selling something that is—ta da—invisible, intangible, and certainly not a product.

- *The Richest Man in Babylon*
  By George S. Clason

Intriguing title, isn't it? The story is just as good. It's all about a simple premise known as 'paying yourself first'. After reading this book, you'll know exactly what that's all about. The questions is: will you do it?

To see the 'Second Bunch of Business Books You Should Read', please visit www.UABSBooks.com.

B) A SMIDGE OF INSPIRATION

- The Bible

-duh!

- *Unstoppable*
  by Cynthia Kersey

-One of the most inspiring books on the market today. Filled with incredibly uplifting and encouraging stories that make you realize there is no excuse for failure if success is what you crave. I cry every time I read it. Guaranteed to be a welcome addition to your personal library. If after you read the story of Legson Kayira you still think you have an excuse for failure… you had better read it again!

- *Forbes Greatest Business Stories of All Time*
  by Daniel Gross

-Too often we forget that even the great moguls of society were, too, once at the bottom of the ladder. From Cyrus McCormick and J.P Morgan to

David Ogilvy and William Gates, these stories will inspire you to go out there and kick some butt. You're going to be in the next edition, right?!

- The Passing of the Night
  by General Robbie Risner

-If General Risner could withstand torture and deprivation for seven years in the Hanoi Hilton during Vietnam… winning an Oscar shouldn't really be all that hard to do. Puts things in perspective, doesn't it? NO EXCUSES, SIR! This book will truly inspire you.

- *Anthem*
  by Ayn Rand

-If you haven't yet read this super-short powerhouse of a book, you absolutely must. It is one of the coolest books ever written on the face of the planet.

- *Unlimited Power & Awaken the Giant Within*
  both by Tony Robbins

-We've all heard of him. How many of us have actually *read* him? There's a good reason why everyone loves him so much. He's good at what he does!

- *How to Sell Your Way Through Life*
  By Napoleon Hill

-I think we could all use a good dose of this, eh?

- *The Law of Success in 16 Lessons* and/or *Law of Success, 21ˢᵗ Century Edition*
  By Napoleon Hill

-What an amazing set of books. It'll take you a while to read the first set (which is two volumes) but they are chock full of amazing inspiration. I read them while I was in Iraq and they helped me plan my triumphant return to the states.

- *Over the Top & See You At the Top*
  both by Zig Zigler

-I saw the Zigmeister speak live at a Get Motivated seminar. I love the guy. Love his books too! So will you.

- *How to Win Friends and Influence People*
  by Dale Carnegie

-Really teaches some basic principles of human psychology. His "Six Principles to Make People Like You" are the cornerstone tenets of influence, and have withstood the test of time, given that the book was published first in 1936.

- *Think & Grow Rich*
  By Napoleon Hill

-Some of the things he talks about are a little left-field, but 99% of it is rock-solid on target. This is a true classic.

C) A TOUCH OF SHOW BUSINESS

Note: read all of these books, but be cautious. As long as you read them with an Unstoppable Artists mentality, you'll be fine.

- True and False
  by David Mamet

-"Heresy and common sense for the actor." A shocking exposé on the acting profession by one of its big players. If you've ever questioned the importance of acting school, if you've ever questioned those silly theater games, or if you simply want to know what everyone is talking about, check this out. I do feel though that he strayed from the tenets espoused in his book by actually opening an acting school [Atlantic Theater Company] but other than that, he's right on the money.

- All You Need To Know About the Movie and TV Business by Gail Resnick and Scott Trost

-Covers *all* careers in Hollywood, from writer to gaffer, and yes, it includes the actor. Discusses some very interesting and enlightening topics. If you plan on working in show business, and especially if you plan on working in film... you should know what everyone's job is, from low guy on the totem pole to Mr. Executive Millionaire.

- How to be a Working Actor: The Insider's Guide to Finding Jobs in Theater, Film, and Television by Mari Lyn Henry & Lynne Rogers

-Very helpful in all aspects of theater as a profession. I should hope, though, that you are striving to be far more than a working actor. You've heard the expression: shoot for the stars; you might hit the moon. Well, same thing here: if you want to be a working actor, you had better be shooting for STAR. Make sense?

- Here's Looking at You: The Actor's Guide to Commercial Print by Scott Powers

-An excellent book for the actor showing how to get involved with this exciting and lucrative (but no less difficult!) part of the business, by the president of Scott Powers Productions in New York City. His class on commercial print modeling is likely the best you will find anywhere. A definite "gosee"! You won't be disappointed.

- How to Make it in Hollywood
  by Linda Buzzell

-As the cover says, "The Ultimate Guide". A fabulous complement to all the business books you've just bought! It shows how to put into action all that you've been learning from this book. Now that you *are* a Theatrical Juggernaut... what do you do? The final section entitled, "All the Right Moves" is a must-read, and will give you much advice on how to do just that. HIGHLY RECOMMENDED.

- *The Job Book II: 100 Days Jobs For Actors*
  by Glenn Alterman

-Still looking for a cool day job? This book was actually one of the factors in helping me decide to start a consulting business for actors. You'll probably find something in here for you too. If not... it will certainly get you thinking.

- Your Film Acting Career
  by M.K. Lewis & Rosemary R. Lewis

-A well-rounded look at a film career from a Hollywood perspective.

- Audition
  by Michael Shurtleff

-"The famed Broadway and Hollywood casting director reveals everything an actor needs to know to get the part." An excellent technique to employ if you have but a few minutes to prepare an audition from sides or scripts given to you on the spot.

- The Complete Film Dictionary
  by Ira Konigsberg

-"The most resourceful sourcebook on the motion picture—as art, technology, and industry—with nearly 4,000 entries on all aspects of filmmaking. More than 250 line drawings and photographs." This is such a cool book. *Anything* (and I mean anything) you ever wanted to know about film is in this HUGE 464-page book.

- Acting Professionally: Raw Facts About Careers in Acting by Robert Cohen

- This was the first book I had ever read on acting professionally, and I'm glad for that! Brief and to the point. Tells you about the acting business point blank, without care for feelings, telling it like it is. Quite an eye-opener.

- *Acting as a Business* by Brian O'Neil

-This book is one of those that must be mentioned simply by virtue of its well-reputed status. It is written from an agent's perspective, as Brian O'Neil is a former agent. It thus complements this book (from an actor's perspective) very nicely. However, its title is misleading because, as we all know by now, acting *is* business, point blank.

- Step By Step to Stand-Up Comedy by Greg Dean

-Foreword by Steve Allen. A great book to help you not only write a standup set, but also to get out there and start performing it. Its Joke Map, Mine, and Prospector system is great for developing new material.

- How to Sell Yourself as an Actor by K Callan

-Although I feel it's incorrect to be of the mindset that you are selling yourself as an actor [you are selling, plain and simple], this book does cover a lot of important topics. You'd be a fool to be without it.

- *An Actor Succeeds*
  by Terrence Hines and Suzanne Vaughan

-A collection of interviews with industry players. Includes two very interesting interviews (with a publicist and an accountant) that itself make the book worth buying. Also includes interviews with casting directors, agents, and others.

- Creating Your Own Monologue
  by Glenn Alterman

-If you can't find a good monologue... write one! You can certainly do it, and it certainly might be a good idea: a) you can tailor the material to yourself, b) you can write about whatever you want, and c) no one will know the difference, guaranteed. This book will help in getting those ideas of yours onto paper.

- Acting in Commercials
  by Joan See

-"A Guide to Auditioning and Performing On Camera." A good coverage of commercials. Covers a lot of basic information, too.

- Breaking Into Commercials
  by Terry Berland & Deborah Ouellette

-Foreword by Jason Alexander of 'Seinfeld'. Another good coverage of commercials. Also covers a lot of basic information.

- *The Art of Voice Acting*
  by James R. Alburger

-"The Craft and Business of Performing for Voice-Over." This book covers… voice-overs!

- *Voice-overs: Putting Your Mouth Where The Money Is*
  by Chris Douthitt

-So does this one! Another good read, offering some different information.

- Next! An Actor's Guide to Auditioning
  by Ellie Kanner, C.S.A., & Paul G. Bens, Jr.

-Foreword by Matt LeBlanc, star of 'Friends'. Written by two prominent casting directors, this book includes some great advice and stories about auditioning. Definitely worth reading.

- *How to Agent Your Agent*
  by Nancy Rainford

-Remember, your agent works for YOU. Don't let them ever forget that. And don't YOU ever forget that either!

- *The Complete Film Production Handbook*
  By Eve Light Honthaner

-If you are producing a film of any sort, this book will show you how to do it, step-by-step, with a 'forms' CD included. Catered primarily to the feature film world, but required reading for any up-and-coming superstar.

- *Digital Filmmaking 101*
  By Dale Newton and John Gaspard

-This book is written for the smaller filmmaker in mind. If you think you are 'just an actor' and are not a filmmaker, then you missed the whole point of this book. Read this one too.

- *Film Directing Fundamentals*
  By Nicholas Proferes

-An absolutely enlightening book. All actors need to read this book. You'll be that much more useful (i.e. non-annoying) on a film set after reading it.

- *Directing Actors*
  By Judith Weston

-If you want to become a better actor... read this book. Learning her techniques will help you learn how to better 'direct yourself'. I read this book while I was in Iraq and was blown away.

- *How to Get the Part... without falling apart*
  By Margie Haber with Barbara Babchick

-A truly wonderful book to help you nail those auditions.

THE ELEVEN CHARACTERISTICS OF UNSTOPPABLE PEOPLE.

11. They are never too important/unimportant for any opportunity.
10. They *never* make excuses for their failure.
9. They take full responsibility for their success.
8. They stay away from the negativity of people going nowhere.
7. They only hang out with other winners.
6. They never let *anyone* tell them that they are going to fail.
5. They make their own rules, and break the rules... all the time.
4. They become the type of person *other* people want to meet.
3. They use their ingenuity to make themselves stand out.
2. They never take no for an answer.
1. They make their own luck.

YOUR BUSINESS, FINANCIAL, & PMA STRATEGY

A) YOU NEED A BUSINESS PLAN, A FINANCIAL PLAN, & A PMA PLAN.

Success—especially success in business—requires a plan. The best plans are those that are written down. Until you write something down, it is just a figment of your imagination. Until you write it down, it is just a thought; a consideration; a passing dream. Once you write it down… it becomes a reality in the making. Once you write it down, it become an actual plan of action that you can use to get you from where you are now to where you are going in the future.

Quite simply, you *must* write down your goals. You *must* have a written business plan. You *must* have a written financial plan. And you *must* have a written PMA plan. For those who need a reminder, PMA stands for publicity, marketing, and advertising.

The first plan—your business plan—is going to help you strategize where you are going in the next ten years and outline how you plan to get there.

The second plan—your financial plan—is going to help you raise, invest, and spend the money you need to set that business plan into action.

The third plan—your PMA plan—is going to help spread the good word about everything you are doing.

It's as simple as 1, 2, 3. You need all three plans in order to ensure lasting success.

B) HOW TO WRITE YOUR BASIC BUSINESS PLAN

Write out on paper exactly where you are, where you are going, and how you are going to get there. Think ten years in advance, and work backwards. Where do you see yourself and your business in ten years? Five years? Three years? Six months? Write it all down.

Then create a strategy to get you from where you are *now* to where you are *going*. Update this at least every three months. Write it up, print it out, and put it everywhere: in your wallet, on your walls, in the bathroom. Use it as a bookmark. Read it before going to bed.

What follows is my simple method for writing out your business plan. I have used this method for the last seven years, and it works. Write your goals down, and they *will* be realized.

MY PLAN

Where am I going?

Write the future. Be positive, upbeat, and confident. Nothing should be wishy-washy. Don't hold back, and be bold. Write everything as if it has already happened, as if it is already foretold. You are the master of your destiny, so unleash the power within you! Start with the words, I AM GOING, and don't lie to yourself! Say *exactly* what you want to happen, and be specific. Be *very* specific.

This section should be updated infrequently.

Where am I now?

Write the past. List all your accomplishments to date in bullet format. Then, explain exactly what all those accomplishments mean.

This section should be updated every three months.

So, how do I get where I am going?

Write the present. How are you going to use your accomplishments to propel yourself into the future of your creation? This section should be written with a six-month timeframe in mind. Write your six-month strives, and say, I AM GOING. Be bold! Finish this section with the following words: "I am going to succeed. I have no other alternative."

This section should be updated every month, always with an updated six-month projection.

C) HOW TO WRITE YOUR BASIC FINANCIAL PLAN

Just like before, you need to start with the end in mind. Where do you see yourself financially in ten years? In five years?

You should be ambitious here. Are you a millionaire? A billionaire? How much money do you have in savings?

Robert Kiyosaki encourages us to create three different milestones: secure, comfortable, and rich. He asks us to write down on paper exactly what financial success means to us. What does it mean to first be secure, then comfortable, and then rich?

What would 'security' mean to you? Paying bills on time? 8 months of living expenses in the bank in an emergency fund? Owning your own house and having a profitable stock market investment portfolio?

What would 'comfort' mean to you? What about 'being rich'?

Then again, work backwards, as before. Figure out what you need to do to realize each of these milestones.

The key always is to write it out. What is going to get you from where you are today to where you are going in the future?

D) HOW TO WRITE YOUR BASIC PMA PLAN

Guess what? You need to once again start... at the end. A publicity, marketing, and advertising plan is no different than any other plan we've discussed. You need to see where you're going in the future... and then work backwards.

If you are going to be written up in the NY Times six months from now... working backwards, you might realize that your best chance of making that happen would probably be sending out press releases once/month starting today, and following through with phone calls each week to their editorial department.

If your mission is to come up with a marketing angle for your acting services... you should plan out the steps you are going to take each week towards that end *today*.

And write it down! You need to write all of this stuff down!

The key to an effective PMA plan is to plan it out generally over the next three years, but really make the next six months as specific as you can. What are you going to be doing each week from a PMA standpoint to further your business endeavors? Write it down... and be consistent in its execution.

As you will certainly understand after you read a bunch of marketing books... consistency rules. The spoils often go to the business who was more consistent in its publicity, marketing, and advertising. It's a simple premise: out of sight, out of mind (and it takes a while before people learn to trust you).

D) PUTTING IT ALL TOGETHER

As mentioned above, you are not likely to succeed by only using *one* of these plans. Nor are any of the plans likely to be effective if you refuse to write them down. You must!

You absolutely must come up with three different plans—a business plan, a financial plan, and a PMA plan—and write each one of them clearly down on paper. An ambitious and clearly written out business plan. An ambitious and clearly written out financial plan. And an ambitious and clearly written out publicity, marketing, and advertising plan. And update them constantly. And put them into action damnit!

When you write these three plans out—after having developed them through some deep thought—you will have before you quite the powerful guide and map. These three documents become your overall business strategy. If you start to put it into action—and refuse to let any obstacles get in your way—you are going to be quite surprised with the pleasantly positive results.

NOTE: If you are seeking assistance in putting together this business strategy; want to learn more about business, marketing, sales, and financing (including the stock market and real estate); and crave the accountability and discipline that we can provide, give us a call at 1-888-YSTARDOM or send an email to info@UnstoppableArtists.com. We'd love to talk with you about our different programs! You may also visit our website at www.UnstoppableArtists.com.

APPENDIX D:

CANNES IT!

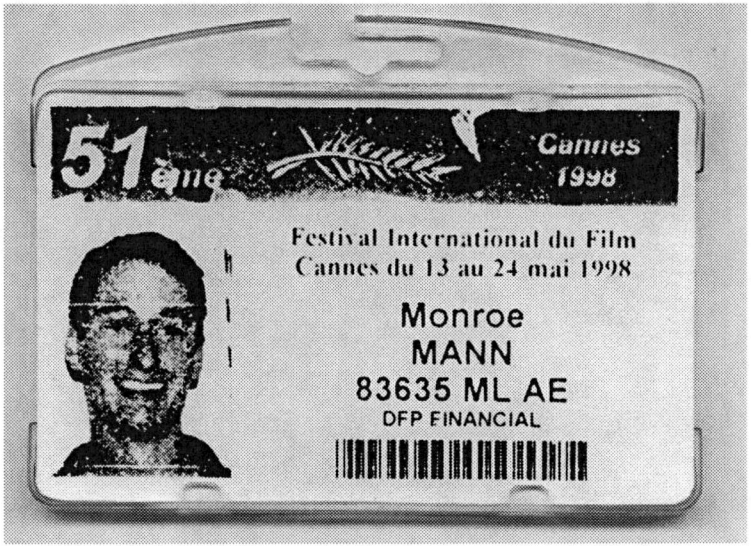

Let this badge be an encouragement to you. This badge is proof that you can do whatever you set your mind to. I crashed the coolest film festival in the world as a no one, and emerged as an 'associate producer'. This is proof to me that one day I will also return to Cannes... as a star. The next time you start to come up with an excuse: CANNES-IT! Just put that doubt to the side, and find another way. There is *always* a way. *Always.* You will find it.

THE AGENT MATRIX™

INTRODUCTION

THE AGENT MATRIX	Light-Weight Agent	Heavy-Weight Agent
Light-Weight Actor		
Heavy-Weight Actor		

What you see above is the unanalyzed UABS Agent Matrix™. Deceptively simple looking, once you come to psychologically understand how it works, your agent problems may very well disappear—or at the very least, you'll finally understand why things either are (or are not) working out for you the way you had hoped.

Similarly, your problems with managers, attorneys, publicists, and anyone else on your team will similarly come into focus, possibly for the first time ever, allowing you to clearly diagnose where you are, where you need to go, and how to go about getting there.

You'll see that it is broken down into two composite parts: down the left column are two types of actors (note that the term 'actor' is being used to describe ALL types of artists), and across the top row are two types of agents (note that the term 'agent' is being used to describe ALL types of industry).

As we move through this discussion, we will be filling in and completing the Agent Matrix™. By the time we are finished, the matrix will be completed, and you will have a clear understanding of how it will positively and irreversibly affect your career in the arts.

I've broken down society (in this case, actors and agents) into only two categories: Light-Weights and Heavy-Weights. Yes, this may seem black and white, but folks, in this world there *are* only two types of people: winners and losers. You are either in one category, or you are in the other. There may be 'shades' of each, but dig to the core of all individuals, and you'll soon see that deep down, their propensity to action is either positive or negative.

With that understood, let's get started.

Light-Weight ACTORs:

THE AGENT MATRIX	Light-Weight Agent	Heavy-Weight Agent
Light-Weight Actor		
Heavy-Weight Actor		

90% of people professing to be actors are in the category of Light-Weight Actors.

In my book, *The Theatrical Juggernaut: The Psyche of the Star*, I refer to them as 'Pretend Actors'. You may also prefer to refer to them as LOSERS! Wannabes! Pessimistic fools! You can call them whatever you want, as long as you understand what they are (so that you don't become one of them).

Light-Weight Actors are those 'artists' who actually believe they are artists, and not businessman; who have unspecific unambitious goals (or worse, no goals at all); who let the business trample over them, rather than trampling over the business; and bottom-line, who ten years from now are going to look back and wonder why they are still starving and unknown.

A pretend actor rarely succeeds on a grand scale and a Light-Weight Actor is on a similarly depressing path.

Many people claim that they are *not* a Light-Weight Actor... but actions speak louder than words. Just look around and you can tell pretty easily who is who. Nine times out of ten, the artist you are looking at is a Light-Weight.

Avoid this person at all costs... and more importantly, do whatever is necessary to NEVER be associated with that category again. You can not afford to be a Light-Weight. Light-Weights are LOSERS and NEVER WIN.

Light-Weight AGENTS:

THE AGENT MATRIX	Light-Weight Agent	Heavy-Weight Agent
Light-Weight Actor		
Heavy-Weight Actor		

Now, 90% of agents also fall into the light-weight category.

They are the EXACT agent equivalent of the Light-Weight Actor.

These 'pretend agents' (who probably were pretend actors to begin with) are unfortunately cluttering up the scene and giving the 10% of great agents out there a bad name.

These Light-Weight Agents are bitter, pessimistic, depressed, unmotivated, and whether they realize it or not, are hoping that you will fail, or at best, don't want you to go any farther than they themselves went with their life.

They have no ambition for themselves, just as they don't want their clients to have any ambition of their own.

I *know* that you know this type of agent, so enough said.

So, then, what happens when you put a Light-Weight Actor and a Light-Weight Agent together?

THE AGENT MATRIX	Light-Weight Agent	Heavy-Weight Agent
Light-Weight Actor	?	
Heavy-Weight Actor		

SIGNAGE. Every Single Time.

They are a perfect match for *eachother* (but not necessarily a perfect match). The Light-Weight Artist has no ambition or true confidence;

And these qualities in turn don't threaten the Light-Weight Agent's own sense of regret and self-consciousness.

The Light-Weight Agent doesn't see a 'star', but rather, only sees little day-player and bit roles that fit the Light-Weight Artist's 'type'. The agent (since the Light-Weight Actor is spellbound under the agent's command) is relieved that the actor isn't going to interfere with his running of the show.

On the other hand, the actor (incorrectly) sees someone who has 'faith' in him, and who is taking active control of his career: The actor (incorrectly) sees in this agent a ticket to stardom (but of course won't dare mention his goals to this agent for fear of reproach). The actor (incorrectly) finally sighs in relief because he doesn't need to deal with the 'business side' anymore, expecting his agent to now do what he could never do to begin with.

Neither of them (deep down) want success. The actor doesn't have the guts to proclaim it; the agent can't get over himself to allow it to happen. They think it's a match made in heaven: it's really just disaster on all fronts. The actor may be signed, but *not in his best interest*.

THE AGENT MATRIX	Light-Weight Agent	Heavy-Weight Agent
Light-Weight Actor	**Non-Star Signage**	
Heavy-Weight Actor		

So… a Light-Weight Actor meeting a Light-Weight Agent will result in signage, yes, but ultimately, NON-STAR SIGNAGE. Which is exactly why I do not necessarily congratulate people when they tell me they just signed with an agent. It very well may be 'Non-Star Signage', or worse, 'Faulty Signage'—which we'll be talking about in just a moment.

HEAVY-Weight AGENTs:

THE AGENT MATRIX	Light-Weight Agent	Heavy-Weight Agent
Light-Weight Actor	Non-Star Signage	
Heavy-Weight Actor		

Now, let's bring another player onto the field: the Heavy-Weight Agent.

As I mentioned, not *all* agents are light-weights. A very rare few, i.e. 10% of all agents, are actually confident, optimistic, with no regrets, and hold the full belief that success in any capacity is possible.

These agents are not agents by default. They are agents because they *love* being an agent, and are doing it because they *wanted to,* and not in any way because they had to. As a result, they only want to deal with actors that are rock-solid on track, and who believe in themselves as much as the agent does in the actor. Just as they want their agency to become more and more well respected in size and reputation, so do they want their actors to succeed beyond their wildest dreams. They only want to deal with Heavy-Weight Actors.

This is the type of agent you want... and need... but *only* if you are a Heavy-Weight Actor, as you'll soon see.

What happens, then, when you put a Light-Weight Actor together with a Heavy-Weight Agent?

THE AGENT MATRIX	Light-Weight Agent	Heavy-Weight Agent
Light-Weight Actor	Non-Star Signage	?
Heavy-Weight Actor		

FAULTY SIGNAGE OR NOTHING AT ALL.

In this case, opposites do NOT attract. In this case, the pessimistic loser Light-Weight Actor will not in any way mesh with the optimistic Heavy-Weight Agent's positive mindset.

When this agent meets an actor, he expects the actor to know exactly what's going on, what he's doing, where he's going, and how he's going to get there. This agent doesn't mess around: it's all about getting to the top and succeeding. This agent doesn't have time to nurture and teach and pick up slack for an actor. This agent is ready to rock and roll... NOW!

This Light-Weight Actor, on the other hand, is a loser. He kowtows to agents and treats them like they are God; he doesn't assert himself and say what needs to be said; and he lets the industry determine his fate, rather than he determining the fate of the industry.

Put these two types of people together (Light-Weight Actor with a Heavy-Weight Agent), and you'll get one of but two things: a) FAULTY SIGNAGE, in which case (a fluke) the actor will be signed (but quickly lost in a sea of Heavy-Weight Actors), or b) NO SIGNAGE, in which case the Heavy-Weight Agent will realize that this actor was not compatible with the agency's way of working.

THE AGENT MATRIX	Light-Weight Agent	Heavy-Weight Agent
Light-Weight Actor	Non-Star Signage	**Faulty/No Signage**
Heavy-Weight Actor		

So... a Light-Weight Actor meeting a Heavy-Weight Agent will either result in FAULTY SIGNAGE, or more often, NOTHING AT ALL.

HEAVY-Weight ARTISTs:

THE AGENT MATRIX	Light-Weight Agent	Heavy-Weight Agent
Light-Weight Actor	Non-Star Signage	Faulty/No Signage
Heavy-Weight Actor		

Now, let's bring the final player onto the field: The Heavy-Weight Actor.

In my book, *The Theatrical Juggernaut: The Psyche of the Star*, I refer to these individuals as Unstoppable Actors, Theatrical Juggernauts, Winners, Future Oscar and Tony Award Winners, etc. They are all Unstoppable Artists.

As with pretend actors, though, the name doesn't matter. It really doesn't matter what you call them, as long as you understand what they are (in this case, so you can *become* one of them). Essentially, they are the few who have the *Psyche of the Star; the people who know where they are going before they get there and who prepare accordingly.* Are you this type of person?

Heavy-Weight Actors have the attitude and the business sense to take charge and make things happen. They know they are going to succeed, and they know how they are going to do it. They break the rules, scorn the idea of luck, do what needs to be done, and make it happen, all the time, everytime. They know so much about running a business that they don't need an agent in order to succeed, but rather, just to make things easier and run more smoothly. The agent is not the end; but rather—merely a *means* to an end.

These actors—these Heavy-Weight Actors—are the superstars of tomorrow. A Heavy-Weight Actor is exactly who you should want to be.

So, let's get back to our scenarios. What happens now when a Heavy-Weight Actor meets a Light-Weight Agent?

THE AGENT MATRIX	Light-Weight Agent	Heavy-Weight Agent
Light-Weight Actor	Non-Star Signage	Faulty/No Signage
Heavy-Weight Actor	?	

FAULTY SIGNAGE OR NOTHING AT ALL

This is the same situation as where a Light-Weight Actor meets a Heavy-Weight Agent, except now, the roles are reversed.

In this case, the Heavy-Weight Actor knows what he wants, and how he's going to get there, but the Light-Weight Agent doesn't believe it. *This* is the situation in which Heavy-Weight Actors most often find themselves at the beginning of their careers: dealing with loser agents, i.e. the vast majority of agents in the world.

Light-Weight Agents, if you'll remember, resent achievers and can't see past their own short-sightedness. They resent those who want to accomplish the impossible, and detest seeing the confidence and ambition they wish they had (when they were younger) in someone else—in someone who is actually pursuing their dreams with a passion.

Light-Weight Agents laugh at people's dreams, and are so blind that they don't see (or don't *want* to see) the future star that's sitting before them. All they see is their own shortcomings all the more clearly.

As a result, the agent usually ends up saying something to bring the actor down like, "Oh, I just can't figure out your type." WELL DUH!! Stars don't have a type; we are STARS! Or something like, "Whoah! Slow down. You need to calm down." Or worse, "If you want to work with me, you need to get a little bit more realistic." Realistic? Realistic? Screw you, you son of a bitch! I am going to the top, and either get on board, or get out of my way! Argh—these light-weights frustrate me so much.

Not only is a Light-Weight Agent not going to push to make that Heavy-Weight Actor's dream a reality, but that agent will perhaps purposefully try to detrimentally hinder the actor's progress, either through disparaging remarks, or worse, through signing the actor, and then purposefully doing nothing for him. How deplorable!

It is hoped that this Heavy-Weight Actor will realize that this agent is a Light-Weight before it's too late and RUN before signing anything. Or, the Heavy-Weight Actor might unfortunately get duped into signing with this Light-Weight Agent (through some fluke), and then wonder why nothing is ever happening. More often than not, though, there will be no chemistry at all between these two individuals, nothing will come of any meeting, and both will be better off for it: the Light-Weight Agent can continue his search for a loser to sign, and the Heavy-Weight Actor can continue his search of destiny, and his Heavy-Weight Agent.

THE AGENT MATRIX	Light-Weight Agent	Heavy-Weight Agent
Light-Weight Actor	Non-Star Signage	Faulty/No Signage
Heavy-Weight Actor	**Faulty/No Signage**	

So... a Heavy-Weight Actor meeting a Light-Weight Agent will either result in FAULTY SIGNAGE, or more often, NOTHING AT ALL.

THE FINAL ANALYSIS:

But there is still one last combination that we haven't yet looked at, that being the pairing of a Heavy-Weight Actor with a Heavy-Weight Agent.

THE AGENT MATRIX	Light-Weight Agent	**Heavy-Weight Agent**
Light-Weight Actor	Non-Star Signage	Faulty/No Signage
Heavy-Weight Actor	Faulty/No Signage	?

This is how stars are born. *This* is a match made in heaven.

The Heavy-Weight Actor comes in, sits down, and lays down the game plan. The Heavy-Weight agent is totally hip to this mentality, and is thrilled to have found someone with such drive and motivation, who is taking charge of his career.

Since the actor knows that he's the CEO, he also realizes that success or failure ultimately falls on *him*, not the agent.

The agent, on a similar note, understands that he is being hired to do a job, with payment on a commission basis.

The actor ambitiously and clearly explains exactly where he is going with his career, and the agent *loves this*, and is going to fight to make it happen—'cause when it does, it will mean millions of dollars for the actor, and hundreds of thousands of dollars for the agent. The actor, thus, is going to do everything he can to make the agent's job as easy as possible. The more work he does to help his agent, the more money they are both going to make.

The agent understands that he is operating on the actor's timetable, and not the other way around, and actually appreciates that he isn't being treated like some God (which is how Light-Weight Actors *always* treat agents, and how Light-Weight Agents preposterously *expect* to be treated by their actors).

The agent also understands that he is working for the actor and is on the *actor's* payroll, and not the other way around. In other words, the agent knows that he is the employee.

Yet, the actor does realize that he and his agent are a *team*. As a result, it's not an antagonistic relationship. On the contrary, the actor simply knows what he wants; and the agent knows he is expected to deliver. And of course, the actor doesn't use the agent as a crutch and just wait for things to happen. Instead, the actor uses his attitude and business skills to propel his own career forward; to give the agent what he needs to do his job.

Bottom line: the Heavy-Weight Actor and the Heavy-Weight Agent are working seamlessly together, diligently progressing towards the same fabulous goal. When the Heavy-Weight Actor says, "I am going to win an Oscar in three years," the Heavy-Weight Agent says, "I know it; in fact, why don't we do it in two!"

THE AGENT MATRIX	Light-Weight Agent	Heavy-Weight Agent
Light-Weight Actor	Non-Star Signage	Faulty/No Signage
Heavy-Weight Actor	Faulty/No Signage	**STAR SIGNAGE**

So... a Heavy-Weight Actor meeting a Heavy-Weight Agent will result in but one thing every single time: POSITIVE STAR SIGNAGE.

It is *this* relationship that you should be striving to develop; First, by becoming a Heavy-Weight Actor; then, by finding that Heavy-Weight Agent to match.

Whenever you meet an agent, and things don't work out, don't necessarily assume it's you. The problem (almost every single time) is that the agent was a Light-Weight, and as you well know by now, Heavy-Weight Actors don't mix with Light-Weight Agents... ever.

This assumes, of course, that you are indeed a Heavy-Weight Actor. Are you? Could you be doing something more to help solidify your Heavy-Weight status? You need to always be striving to become more Heavy-Weight tomorrow than you were today. 'Cause maybe—just maybe—you're not a Heavy-Weight yet. And if not, you need to realize this and fix this *before* you start approaching the Heavy-Weight Agents!

If you have drive and determination, though, you *will* inevitably become a Heavy-Weight Actor, and THEN, with patience and perseverance, you *will* find that Heavy-Weight Agent to complete the puzzle.

Then, *and only then*, will you live happily ever after... as a STAR!

Conclusion to the Agent Matrix:

Here is the completed matrix. Study it. Learn it. Live it:

THE AGENT MATRIX	Light-Weight Agent	Heavy-Weight Agent
Light-Weight Actor	**Non-Star Signage**	**Faulty/No Signage**
Heavy-Weight Actor	**Faulty/No Signage**	STAR SIGNAGE

I hope you now understand the true situation that exists between actors and agents.

I hope you see now that it's indisputably better to be an unsigned Heavy-Weight Actor than to be a signed Light-Weight Actor going nowhere.

If you are a Heavy-Weight Actor (and I'm assuming you are, or are striving to be), then any relationship with a Light-Weight Agent will only serve to bring you down. Even though you'll have the prestige of telling everyone that you're signed, you'll actually be worse off than before you were signed.

As you can see, finding the right agent requires a LOT of effort on the part of the actor. It requires that you have the Psyche of the Star, so that you have the guts to proclaim your future; it requires that you have standards which you will not compromise; it requires that you have an incredible amount of patience as you meet with Light-Weight Agent after Light-Weight Agent until you finally hit pay dirt with that Heavy-Weight Agent you had been waiting for; it requires that you know and understand all facets of business better than your competition. Finding the right agent requires HARD WORK!

And, finally, as a follow up to what we discussed just a moment ago, please don't just automatically assume that you ARE a Heavy-Weight Actor. That's the problem will most Light-Weights: They think they're on the high road to success, but they're not; and often they don't even know the difference between the two types of artists. Take accountability constantly by always asking yourself: AM I A LIGHT-WEIGHT (Pretend Actor), or am I a Heavy-Weight (Unstoppable Actor)? Would a Heavy-Weight be doing this? What would a Heavy-Weight do? Realize that at any given time, you might be displaying some elements of both. During the day, you might move back and forth between the two. The key is to be Heavy-Weight *all the time*. It's hard to do, but what you must strive for.

In the end, of course, the choice is yours: am I satisfied being a Light-Weight, or am I willing to sacrifice in order to become a Heavy-Weight? Truly, *that* is what is ultimately going to determine your fate. YOUR CHOICES TODAY!

Only if you are a Heavy-Weight Actor can you ever hope to find a Heavy-Weight Agent who will truly understand you and earnestly help take you where you want to go. If you are not a Heavy-Weight Actor with uncompromising standards actively searching for that ever elusive Heavy-Weight Agent, the only other option is to spend the rest of your life cursing this business as a Light-Weight Pretend Actor wondering why it just never worked out…

And wouldn't that just suck?

Avoid that. At any and all costs.

Become that Heavy-Weight you know you can be.

Your future depends on it.

Truly.

It does.

Praise for Monroe Mann and Unstoppable Artists Business School

(...or, why you should become a student!)

"To make it big, you need the Real Deal. Mr. Mann is the Real Deal."
– Jay Conrad Levinson, author of Guerrilla Marketing, with over 14 million copies sold worldwide.

"If you're ready to improve your chances of success in work and in life, you'd be wise to get 'battle-ready' at Monroe's boot camp for winners."
– Bob Fraser, author of You Must Act, and Emmy-recognized writer/ producer of Benson & Full House.

"If I can learn something from Monroe Mann and his school... then you certainly can too." *– Lorraine Serabian, Tony-Nominated Actress, Film & Theatre Acting Coach, and student, Unstoppable Artists*

"Monroe Mann is an explosion of positive energy – just sitting in the room with him will get you excited about your future again!" *–* **Joan Ellis, Tony-Nominated Actress, Film & Theatre Acting Coach, and student, Unstoppable Artists**

"Using the techniques I learned at UABS, I finally took my career into my own hands. I quit my so-called 'survival job', and I am now a full-time working actor and producer. I have been interviewed on *Carson Daly*, in *New York Magazine*, at *Broadway.com*, and others... All within months after meeting Monroe Mann. Reading *The Theatrical Juggernaut* and joining Unstoppable Artists awakened within me something that I already knew, but forgot. The only thing standing between myself and greatness is... myself. I now have the vision, the tools, and the drive. Thanks Monroe! See you at the Top!" – **Douglas C. Williams, Actor, and founder of Three Feet From Gold Productions**, www. DouglasCWilliams.com

"Since becoming a student of the Unstoppable Artists Business School in 2002, I self-produced my very own one-man cabaret show which ran to sold out crowds in 2002 for three months at NYC's famous Don't Tell Mama. I was nominated for a 2003 MAC award for best male debut, and received rave reviews in many national publications as well as praise in Backstage as one of the best debuts of 2002. I also produced and recorded my first CD entitled Scot Wisniewski: A Classic Christmas on Independent Records. The CD sold out in the 2002 Christmas season, and received rave reviews in every major theater publication in NYC. This past year, I was also hired for two commercial print modeling layouts in Training Magazine. As a bonus, I was recently recognized by my alma mater Keuka College with a lengthy article published in their quarterly magazine about my success. All because of the school." – **Scot Wisniewski, Actor, Producer, and founder of Independent Records**, www.ScotW.com

"When I arrived at the school, I was a steadily working commercial actor (Novartis, Sony, Xerox, Ovaltine, Breck Shampoo, etc) with an average of a booking each week. Using the techniques I learned at Unstoppable Artists, I'm now taking it all to the next level. Now armed with stronger business & marketing tools from the UABS, I am now approaching the market more specifically and creating an entertainment TV dog show which I will host with my dog. I also started my own company, Leashes

& Lovers, which has afforded me interviews in many publications, including Glamour UK. Thanks Monroe!" – **Sheryl Matthys, Actress, and founder of Leashes & Lovers,** www.LightsCameraTalent.com

"Getting involved with Unstoppable Artists Business School was the best investment I have ever made in my career... Using his techniques, I just got written up in *People Magazine* and just appeared on *Entertainment Tonight* regarding a short film I produced myself called *The Albino Code*, which is a spoof on *The DaVinci Code*. Monroe's school is exactly what I had been looking for." – **Dennis Hurley, Actor, and Producer,** WATCH THE FILM: www.AlbinoCode.com

"I'd been chugging along steadily, but slowly in my acting career for four years. Little I was doing was having the desired effect on my progress. I made excuses, invested too much in the self-defeating idea of "luck", and wallowed in desperation and uncertainty about the future. The class was just what the doctor ordered. Further expanding on principles and ideas introduced in his book, the course was jet-fuel propulsion. Monroe's iron-clad work ethic and unyielding spirit catapulted me to re-acquainting myself with my own potential. And that potential, that endless drive I always had deep within me, has done more for my career in the past three months than the prior years put together. Monroe's book *The Theatrical Juggernaut* and his school's business program were just what the doctor ordered, right at the perfect time in my life. Before I took his program, I was at the lowest of lows in my career. Everything seemed hopeless, useless. I questioned what the hell I was doing and who I was fooling. Taking Monroe's program and reading his book got me out of my futile, indulgent rut in a BIG way and gave my butt the swift, full-on kick it ever so needed. Now I'm on overdrive. Using the techniques I learned at UABS, I've approached my career from a completely new angle & with a refreshing new attitude—and it has made such a mountain of difference. For example, during the last week of his class I booked a principle role on NBC's *ER*. Enough said. But I'll say a few more things. I also signed with an agent and found a new management group. My website went up at that time as well. Most recently, I booked my second

Random House audio book. I thank Monroe for all this. I needed the kick in the ass, and the road map to show me a way." – **From Erik Davies, Actor, and Producer,** <u>www.ErikDavies.com</u>

"Monroe Mann is the most positive and inspirational person I have met in New York City. If anyone has ever told you that your dreams are too big and your success is based on luck, then you really must meet Monroe, read his book The Theatrical Juggernaut-The Psyche of the Star, and take his class at UABS. You will be inspired, motivated, and rightly convinced that there is nothing in your way. In the past month, I have been called in for numerous independent films, have started writing a book, and have begun submitting grant proposals for my own arts education organization! I have learned that my future is made by ME, not by "the perfect agent", not by casting directors, and most definitely not by luck! UABS is a real business school, and not like most fluff "business for actors" classes offered. This is the real deal! I have learned how to market, advertise and publicize my services as an actress, dancer, and writer—to accentuate and show off my unique qualities and characteristics—to set myself apart from every other performer. Perhaps most importantly, Monroe is a living example of what he teaches—he talks the talk and walks the walk. He literally practices what he preaches and does so with passion! Monroe not only teaches his students, but he fully believes in all their dreams and sincerely wants to help them and see them succeed. Become UNSTOPPABLE—take his class now!" – **Tamara Kosh, Actor, Dancer, and Founder of Arts United,** <u>www.TamaraKosh.com</u>

"Using the techniques I learned at Unstoppable Artists, I started pre-production on a jazz cd, I am in the process of putting together my first one-woman show, and my screenplay—a romantic comedy entitled *If You Want to Make the Gods Laugh*—is now in rehearsals for a reading. In addition, I am proud to have added an alumni of incredibly talented and business-savvy individuals to my personal network. Let me backtrack: I read Monroe Mann's first book The Theatrical Juggernaut while on sabbatical in California. I was blown away! It was such a wake up call, and a revelation! One of my favorite lines in this highly inspirational and educational book is "The best time to give it your all is when you've got nothing left to give." Well, I was exactly at that point, so I took the leap of faith upon returning to New York, and enrolled at UABS. It turned out to be an intensely thought-provoking and truly business-enhancing class. For starters, Mr. Mann sets forth the importance of running your business as an entrepreneur. He helps you create your personal business strategy and personal style, and develops within you an understanding of PMA (Publicity, Marketing, & Advertising) and how to incorporate it all into your business strategy. He expounds on the importance of visibility, shows you how to gain and keep clarity in your business through good financial practices, and of course, he talks about attitude. Not only is Mr. Mann an incredibly positive and unstoppable force in person, but he is also a wonderful teacher and coach. In fact, I would take the program again, just to brush up, reinforce, and refine all of the invaluable business techniques he imparted. My business and personal styles are forever changed. Monroe's school has and will continue to change the course of my life: I finally know that I am on my way. Put a kick in your pants and get your dreams up and off the ground: Enroll at UABS! I recommend Unstoppable Artists for anyone who wants to enhance their business "know-how," and who is truly serious about success. Thank you UABS and Monroe Mann!" – **Emilie Bonsant, Actor, and Producer,** www. EmilieBonsant.com

"I took Monroe's program in Feb 2002. I found it practical, inspiring and empowering. After the program, I begin auditioning like crazy with an actual business plan and as a result, I quickly found myself doing my first Equity tour (Kiss Me Kate), at the Carousel Theatre in Ohio, playing one of the leads: Gangster one, who sings Brush Up Your Shakespeare. Soon after, I booked another Equity show from which I gained my Equity card. Thanks Monroe." – **Arthur Brown, Actor,** www.ArthurSBrown.com.

"Using the techniques I learned at Unstoppable Artists, I accomplished more things in a month than I had in the entire previous year. Monroe Mann, a fireball of positive energy and enthusiasm, literally cheered me out of my complacency and got me going. His book *The Theatrical Juggernaut* gave me so many great ideas and such inspiration that I started to put it all into practice right away. One of his slogans—No Excuses!—has become my mantra and, since then, I have effortlessly gone from show to show to show. I would follow this man anywhere! This man will change your life AND your career!" – **Charlotte Patton, Actress, and Producer,** www.CharlottePatton.com

"I am sooooo glad that I had the good brains to take your class, read your book, and leave the competition in the dust! Your class is nothing short of amazing. I walked away with the tools to get started on planning my own future and being my own boss." – **Ginger Leilani Chapin, Actress,** www.GingerLeilani.com

"Monroe's business classes are right out of a business school curriculum. Monroe is the *only* teacher who dares actors to take control of their careers as the business that it is. The focus is on marketing, finance, publicity, advertising, and developing a pioneer, groundbreaking mindset! The expansion of Unstoppable Artists will only serve to benefit the artistic community and the city as a whole as Monroe Mann encourages performers to remember that they are running their greatest venture: their businesses." – **Daphne Shawn, Actress,** www.DaphneShawn.com

"While I was taking his class at UABS, I formed my own production company Joey Vegas Productions, which went on to produce wrote the award-winning short film, *The Lilac Papers* starring two-time Emmy-winning actress Stephanie Braxton... and me! One feature film later as well as speaking roles on *Law & Order: Criminal Intent*, *Rescue Me* and numerous commercials & industrials, I am now flying high as a successful actor/writer/filmmaker and person! Having Monroe Mann in your court is a must for anyone. I highly recommend him if you are tired of wishing & hoping. My motivation, know-how, & success is all a direct result of being coached by Monroe Mann at UABS. Monroe... your name is now in my acceptance speech for my Tony, Emmy, Oscar & Grammy.'" – **Jeff Goldstein, Actor,** www.JeffGoldstein.com

"I expected Monroe's class to be informative and to give me a jumpstart on getting excited about my career again. Not only did the class exceed my expectations, it blew me away! By teaching the importance of both business sense and consistent positive attitude, Monroe has challenged the myth that 'good acting' is the most important success tool." – **Julie Delman, Actress**

"I'm sure that not so long from now, I will look back on Unstoppable Artists Business School and be able to say that it marked the turning point in my career. I spent more years than I can care to tell, aimlessly wandering through my 'acting career' due to a lack of good, practical information. However, with what I learned in this course I now have the tools to ensure success. Instead of waiting around for it, I am going to make it happen, and when that day arrives (and it WILL), I am prepared. If your career is not what you want it to be, not what you KNOW it can be, perhaps all you need is a little business to get you on track. If you don't take care of your business, you can't take care of your art. Just a little something to think about. Sign up today!" – **Craig Rehnke, Actor**

"Thank you Monroe! The whole class is quite life altering and it is making some new grooves in the brain… Interestingly, this new world is already opening up to me. Extremely successful people are coming out of the woodwork to mentor me!" – **Stephanie Peterson, Actress**

"I am so so very happy that I invested in your school. You are a God send! I have been longing for something like this for quite sometime. I am thrilled to start implementing these principles into my business. Your school is different from everything else out there because you practice what you preach! Like most of us, you're in it to win it, and you certainly know what it takes." – **Nanya-Akuki Goodrich, Actress**

TIRED OF THE STRUGGLE? SO WERE WE.

Learn Business… Become Successful.
Our students have.

Unstoppable Artists Business School, the company that inspired this book, is the only school for artists offering you the business skills, marketing know-how, and financial savvy to complement your talents. We offer business classes, workshops, and one-on-one mentoring for the ambitious and serious artist. Just us today. Artists *need* to learn this stuff. It makes success easier. Your future really may depend on it.

We encourage you to please check out our website at UnstoppableArtists.com, to call us at 1-888-YSTARDOM (Why not!), or to send us an email at info@UnstoppableArtists.com for more information. There are artists… and then there are Unstoppable Artists. Which would you rather be? We're the kick in the pants you've been looking for!"

Want to succeed sooner rather than later? Then you ___need___ to register now for Business Class or our one-on-one Mentoring Program. You'll be glad you did.

Contact us today!
www.UnstoppableArtists.com
Info@UnstoppableArtists.com
1-888-YSTARDOM (Why not?!)

Looking for the books that are going to help
catapult your career onto the fast-track?

Look no further!

Check out our
Unstoppable Artists
Business School
BOOK STORE!

Hundreds of books that are approved with the UABS stamp of approval.

www.UABSBooks.com

(powered by Amazon)

Check us out today!

100% Money Back Guarantee

If you are not totally satisfied with this book, simply return it with your receipt to the following address. We will refund your money, no questions asked,
and welcome any comments for improvement:

RETURNS
PO BOX 3
PORT CHESTER, NY 10573

NOW... WHERE TO PUT ALL OF THESE WONDERFUL QUOTES?

He who opens a school door, closes a prison.
—**Victor Hugo**

Flaming enthusiasm, backed up by horse sense and persistence, is the quality that most frequently makes for success.
—**Dale Carnegie**

Success is going from failure to failure without a loss of enthusiam.
—**Winston Churchill**

Dreams will get you nowhere; a good kick in the pants will take you a long way.
—**Baltasar Gracian**

Hold fast to dreams, for if dreams die, life is a broken winged bird that cannot fly.
—**Langston Hughes**

Don't worry about people stealing your ideas. If your ideas are any good, you'll have to ram them down people's throats.
—**Howard Aiken**

I couldn't wait for success, so I went ahead without it.
—**Jonathan Winters**

There are two kinds of companies, those that work to try to charge more and those that work to charge less. We will be the second.
—**Jeff Bezos**

I am certainly not one of those who need to be prodded. In fact, if anything, I am the prod.
—**Winston Churchill**

Obstacles are those frightful things you see when you take your eyes off your goal.
—**Henry Ford**

Don't let your ego get too close to your position, so that if your position gets shot down, your ego doesn't go with it.
—Colin Powell

Creativity is allowing yourself to make mistakes. Art is knowing which ones to keep.
—Scott Adams

There are some days when I think I'm going to die from an overdose of satisfaction.
—Salvador Dali

An artist is someone who produces things that people don't need to have but that he - for some reason - thinks it would be a good idea to give them.
—Andy Warhol

The artist is nothing without the gift, but the gift is nothing without work.
—Emile Zola

The roots of education are bitter, but the fruit is sweet.
—Aristotle
Great minds have purpose, others have wishes.
—Washington Irving

Until one is committed, there is hesitancy, the chance to draw back, always ineffectiveness. Concerning all acts of initiative (and creation), there is one elementary truth the ignorance of which kills countless ideas and splendid plans.

The moment one definitely commits oneself, then providence moves too. All sorts of things occur to help one that would never otherwise have occurred. A whole stream of events issues from the decision, raising in one's favor all manner of unforeseen incidents and meetings and material assistance, which no man could have dreamed would have come his way.
—W. H. Murray

Whatever you can do, or dream you can, begin it. Boldness has genius, power and magic in it. Begin it now.
—Goethe

The most important single ingredient in the formula of success is knowing how to get along with people.
—Theodore Roosevelt

We fail because deep inside we want to.
We rise when we have no alternatives.
Extinguish your alternatives
And you have no where to go but UP!
—Nirvikar Dahiya

Education is an admirable thing, but it is well to remember from time to time that nothing that is worth knowing can be taught.
—Oscar Wilde

It is what a man thinks of himself that really determines his fate.
—Henry David Thoreau

I was told to avoid the business all together because of the rejection. People would say to me, 'Don't you want to have a normal job and a normal family?' I guess that would be good advice for some people, but I wanted to act.
—Jennifer Aniston

The greatest test of courage on earth is to bear defeat without losing heart.
—Robert Green Ingersoll

The hardest victory is victory over self.
—Aristotle

Things work out best for the people
Who make the best out of the way things work out.
—Author unknown

To climb steep hills requires a slow pace at first.
—**William Shakespeare**

Always bear in mind that your own resolution to succeed is more important than any one thing.
—**Abraham Lincoln**

You see things that are and say "Why?"
But I dream things that never were and say "Why not?"
—**George Bernard Shaw**

The history of the world is full of men who rose to leadership by sheer force of self-confidence, bravery, and tenacity.
—**Mohandas Ghandi**

Every morning in Africa, a gazelle awakens.
He has only one thought on his mind:
To be able to run faster than the fastest lion.
If he cannot, then he will be eaten.

Every morning in Africa a lion awakens.
He has only one thought on his mind:
To be able to run faster than the slowest gazelle.
If he cannot, he will die of hunger.

Whether you choose to be a gazelle or a lion is of no consequence.
It is enough to know that with the rising of the sun, you must run.
And you must run faster than you did yesterday or you will die.
This is the race of life.
—**African Proverb**

The ladder of success is best climbed by stepping on the rungs of opportunity.
—**Ayn Rand**

There is no shortcut to winning and success. There is only getting started and sticking with it.
—**Author unknown**

I rate enthusiasm even above professional skill.
—Edward Appleton

One of the rules of caution is not to be too cautious.
—Bahya ibn Paquda

It is effort that makes the inevitable come to pass.
—Oliver Wendell Holmes

To worry about what you don't have is to waste what you do have.
—Author unknown

You cannot build a reputation on what you are going to do.
—Henry Ford

We each have only enough strength to complete those assignments that we are fully convinced are important.
—Goethe

Just because something doesn't do what you planned it to do doesn't mean it's useless.
—Thomas A. Edison

Some people follow their dreams,
Others hunt them down and beat them mercilessly into submission.
—Neil Kendall

In the simplest terms, a leader is one who knows where she wants to go, and gets up and goes.
—John Eskine

Time is the scarcest resource and unless it is managed nothing else can be managed.
—Peter Drucker

My mother said to me,
'If you become a soldier, you'll be a general;
if you become a monk, you'll end up as the pope.'
Instead, I became a painter and wound up as Picasso.
—**Pablo Picasso**

Suffer now and live the rest of your life as a champion.
—**Muhammed Ali**

I used my imagination...
To make the grass whatever color I wanted it to be.
—**Whoopi Goldberg**

It takes a lot of courage to show your dreams to someone else.
—**Erma Bombeck**

The darkest moments of our lives are not to be buried and forgotten.
Rather they are a memory to be called upon for inspiration to remind
us of the unrelenting human spirit and our capacity to overcome the
intolerable.
—**Lance Armstrong**

It is at precisely the moment,
When we are at our lowest ebb,
That the tide begins to turn.
—**Author unknown**

Those who succeed are the efficient few. They are the few who have
the ambition and will power to develop themselves.
—**Author unknown**

It's hard to beat a person who never gives up.
—**Babe Ruth**

Nobody is ever old until the day
That dreams are replaced by regrets...
—**Jannie Putter**

Keep adding, keep walking, keep advancing; do not stop, do not turn back, do not turn from the straight road.
—St. Augustine

The toughest thing about success is that you've got to keep on being a success.
—Irving Berlin

The secret of success is constancy to purpose.
—Disraeli

Do the little things well now. In time, great things will be presented to you, waiting to be done.
—Persian Proverb

You gotta have a dream.
If you never have a dream,
How are you gonna have a dream come true?
—Rogers and Hammerstein

The more that learn to read the less learn how to make a living. That's one thing about a little education. It spoils you for actual work. The more you know the more you think somebody owes you a living.
—Will Rogers

Never measure the height of a mountain until you have reached the top.
—Dag Hammerskjold

To conquer without risk is to triumph without glory.
—El Cid

If we had no winter,
The spring would not be so pleasant;
If we did not sometimes taste of adversity,
Prosperity would not be so welcome.
—Anne Bradstreet

Winners make goals, others make excuses.
—**Author unknown**

Boldness, more boldness, and always boldness!
—**Georges Jacques Danton**

Show me someone who has done something worthwhile, and I'll show you someone who has overcome adversity.
—**Lou Holtz**

Try, try, try, and keep on trying is the rule that must be followed to become an expert in anything.
—**W. Clement Stone**

The best way to make your dreams come true is to wake up.
—**Paul Valery**

Press on: Nothing in the world can take the place of perseverance.
—**Calvin Coolidge**

No one can give you better advice than yourself.
—**Cicero**

Whatever you are by nature, keep to it; never desert you line of talent. Be what nature intended you for and you will succeed.
—**Sydney Smith**

There is nothing good or bad, but thinking makes it so.
—**Shakespeare**

The measure of success is not whether you have a tough problem to deal with, but whether it's the same problem you had last year.
—**John Foster Dulles**

The truth doesn't hurt unless it ought to.
—**Author unknown**

The future belongs to those who prepare for it.
—Emerson

It usually takes me more than three weeks to prepare a good impromptu speech.
—Mark Twain

Most people never run far enough on their first wind,
To find out if they've got a second.
Give your dreams all you've got,
And you'll be amazed at the energy that comes out of you.
—William James

Courage is believing in yourself, and that is something no one can teach you.
—El Cordobes

Knowledge of what is possible is the beginning of success.
—Santayana

The fastest way to succeed is to look as if you're playing by somebody else's rules, while quietly playing by your own.
—Michael Korda

An average person puts only 25% of their energy and ability into their work. The world takes its hat off to those who put more than 50% capacity, and stands on its head for those few and far between souls who devote 100%.
—Andrew Carnegie

True courage is like a kite: a contrary wind raises it higher.
—Author unknown

Our plans miscarry because they have no aim. When you don't know what harbor you're aiming for, no wind is the right wind.
—Seneca

Success is rooted in vision. Always affirm that you will succeed.
—**Author unknown**

We know what happens to people who stay in the middle of the road. They get run over.
—**Aneurin Bevan**

If there is no wind, row.
—**Latin proverb**

The secret of success is to be ready when your opportunity comes.
—**Disraeli**

So many of our dreams at first seem impossible, then they seem improbable, and then, when we summon the will, they soon become inevitable.
—**Christopher Reeve**

A hero is no braver than an ordinary person, but he is braver five minutes longer.
—**Emerson**

You must have courage, whatever the test, however many times you fall, stand up just once more.
—**Author unknown**

There are two ways of meeting difficulties: alter the difficulties, or alter the way you meet them.
—**Phyllis Bottome**

The greatest hurdle is convincing yourself that what you want is possible.
—**Author unknown**

Victory belongs to the most persistent.
—**Author unknown**

I think everyone should go to college and get a degree and then spend six months as a bartender and six months as a cabdriver. Then they would really be educated.
—Al McGuire

You must act as if it is impossible to fail.
—Ashanti Proverb

In the middle of difficulty, lies opportunity.
—Einstein

In a calm sea everyone is a pilot. Strength is proven in adversity.
—English Proverb

Successful people aren't those without problems, they're those who've learned to solve their problems.
—Author unknown

When I was young, I observed that nine out of every 10 things I did failed, so I did 10 time more work.
—George Bernard Shaw

Live your life as an Exclamation rather than an explanation.
—Bob Newton

Treat people as if they were what they ought to be,
And you help them to become what they are capable of being.
—Goethe

Fools scatter about their many attributes,
The wise keep such within;
A piece of straw floats upon the surface of water
A precious gemstone sinks to the bottom!
Therefore, it is best to disregard the seen
And concentrate upon the unseen.
Only within the latter may riches be found.
—**Ancient Greek parable**

Every person you meet knows something you don't,
Learn from them.
—**H. Jackson Brown**

Lack of will power has caused more failure
Than lack of intelligence or ability.
—**Flower A. Newhouse**

Victory belongs to the most persistent.
—**Author unknown**

Make the most of every failure. Fall forward.
—**Author unknown**

Only those who will risk going too far
Can possibly find out how far one can go.
—**T.S. Eliot**

There will come a time when you believe everything is finished.
That will be the beginning.
—**Louis L'Amour**

It is not the critic who counts,
Not that man who points out how the strong man stumbled,
Or where the doers of deeds could have done them better.
The credit belongs to the man who is actually in the arena;
Whose face is marred by the dust and sweat and blood;
Who strives valiantly; who errs and comes short again and again
Who knows the great enthusiasms, the great devotions
And spends himself in a worthy cause; who, at the best,
Knows in the end the triumph of high achievement;
And who, at worst if he fails, at least fails while daring greatly,
So that his place shall never be with those cold and timid souls
Who know neither victory nor defeat.
—**Theodore Roosevelt**

If God intended for today to be perfect,
He would not have invented tomorrow.
—**Author unknown**

QUIT YOUR WAY TO THE TOP!
Quit complaining!
Quit blaming the past for your present!
Quit making excuses!
Quit procrastinating!
Quit blaming others if things don't turn out right!
Quit being close-minded!
Quit doubting yourself!
Quit being afraid!
Quit saying "If only"!
Quit basing your life on what other people say or think!
Quit refusing to get up after a fall!
Who ever said a quitter can't win?
You just need to choose what to quit on!
—**Pete Zafra**

I don't use drugs, my dreams are frightening enough.
—**M. C. Escher**

Never give in--never, never, never, never, in nothing great or small, large or petty, never give in except to convictions of honor and good sense. Never yield to force; never yield to the apparently overwhelming might of the enemy."
—**Winston Churchill**

The greater the obstacle, the more the glory in overcoming it.
—**Moliere**

Losers look what they are going through.
Winners look where they are going to."
—**Jarred Britany**

Failure is only the opportunity to more intelligently begin again.
—**Henry Ford**

A man's dreams are an index to his greatness.
—**Author unknown**

If you focus on results, you will never change.
If you focus on change, you will get results.
—**Jack Dixon**

A ship in a harbor is safe, but that's not what ships are built for.
—**Author unknown**

One hundred percent of the shots you don't take, don't go in.
—**Wayne Gretzky**

When you get into a tight place and it seems you can't go on,
Hold On!
For that's just the place and the time,
That the tide will turn.
—**Harriet Beecher Stowe**

If you don't know where you're going,
Any road will get you there.
—**Lewis Carroll**

Whether you think you can or you can't, you're right.
—Henry Ford

Most people give up just when they're about to achieve success.
They quit on the one yard line.
They give up at the last minute of the game,
One foot from a winning touchdown.
—H. Ross Perot

Obstacles are put in our way to see if we really want something
Or we just thought we did.
—Author unknown

Those who say it can't be done
Are being passed by those doing it.
—Author unknown

I have learned that success is to be measured
Not so much by the position that one has reached in life,
But by the obstacles which they have overcome while trying to succeed.
—Booker T. Washington

It is something to be able to paint a particular picture,
Or to carve a statue, and so to make a few objects beautiful;
But it is far more glorious to carve and paint
The very atmosphere and medium through which we look.
To affect the quality of the day, that is the highest of the arts.
—Thoreau

There is more in us than we know.
If we can be made to see it, perhaps, for the rest of our lives,
We will be unwilling to settle for less.
—Kurt Hahn

The impossible only takes a little longer to achieve.
—Author unknown

It is not the strongest of the species that survives,
Nor the most intelligent,
But the most responsive to change.
—**Darwin**

I haven't failed. I've found 10,000 ways that won't work.
—**Benjamin Franklin**

Remember that someone, somewhere, is practicing, and when you meet him, he will win.
—**Edward Macauley**

If you would hit the mark, you must aim a little above it.
—**Longfellow**

I realized early on that success in acting as a career was tied to not giving up and having an unquenchable thirst and positive attitude towards this business. Most people who started out in this business felt all of the unavoidable rejection, took it personally, and not having much talent to begin with, just gave up and went on to other things. I realized early on that this was a business like any other, and I treated it as such. I spent years doing extra work for $2 an hour and getting a few residuals and plays here and there, but the people I met on-set and the lessons I learned during the lean times paid off when I got in the union and started auditioning for bigger roles. If you simply didn't give yourself anything to fall back on, kept a professional mindset, cultivated your talent, learned at every opportunity, and most importantly, no matter what your family or your wife said, just didn't give up, you would outlast the people who came in on the bus with you and be a success. It happened to me and has happened time and time again to many other talented actors. Talent isn't enough, though, it's your professional mindset that gets most of the work for you.
—**Harrison Ford**

Hire my son. Give him a part in your production.
—**Carolyn Mann, my mother** ☺

Reader comments are always welcome, and are actively encouraged.

Please feel free to contact me—Monroe Mann—at:

roe@UnstoppableArtists.com
www.UnstoppableArtists.com
1-888-YSTARDOM (1-888-978-2736)
Why? Because you deserve it. ☺

TIRED OF THE STRUGGLE? SO WERE WE.

Learn Business… Become Successful.
Our students have.

Unstoppable Artists Business School, the company that inspired this book, is the only school for artists offering you the business skills, marketing know-how, and financial savvy to complement your talents. We offer business classes, workshops, and one-on-one mentoring for the ambitious and serious artist. Join us today. Artists *need* to learn this stuff. It makes success easier. Your future really may depend on it.

We encourage you to please check out our website at UnstoppableArtists.com, to call us at 1-888-YSTARDOM (Why not!), or to send an email to info@UnstoppableArtists.com for more information.

There are artists… and then there are Unstoppable Artists. Which would you rather be? We're the kick in the pants you've been looking for!

Want to succeed sooner rather than later? Then you _need_ to register now for Business Class or our one-on-one Mentoring Program. You'll be glad you did.

Contact us today!
www.UnstoppableArtists.com
Info@UnstoppableArtists.com
1-888-YSTARDOM (Why not?!)

LaVergne, TN USA
21 November 2010

205774LV00006B/37/A